What people are sa~

The Pa*'

Speaking as a Freemasc   .ate Robert Sachs'
work in this book because .   .umber of issues central
to Freemasonry: civil coexist.   .e integration of spiritual and
worldly wisdom, and respect for the world's diverse religious
and philosophical traditions. These are perennial matters to
humanity, and it seems every generation must rediscover not
only their importance, but also the relevant wisdom passed on
to us from previous generations. Sachs' integration of wisdom
from Washington and the Buddha is both deeply insightful and
thoroughly practical. It amounts to a master worker's tool kit for
being compassionately proactive and responsive amid the social
complexities of our increasingly diverse and interconnected
world.

CR Dunning, author of *Contemplative Masonry*

Conscious leadership begins with an idea that freedom and
peace are not only possible, but are our inherent nature as human
beings. Robert Sachs' *The Path of Civility* gives our mind a reason
to accept what our heart already knows – that passion, love, and
compassion is the great healer of life. The power to passionately
and compassionately love into civility lives within each of us.
Thank you, Robert, for this gift to humanity.

Dr. Darren Weissman, originator of The LifeLine Technique and
author of *The Heart of the Matter*

Robert Sachs has written an extremely timely and pertinent
book, because we urgently need to bring civility back into our
personal interactions and political discourse.

Tim Freke, author of *Soul Story*

The Path of Civility

Perfecting the Lessons of a President by
Applying the Wisdom of a Buddha

The Path of Civility

Perfecting the Lessons of a President by Applying the Wisdom of a Buddha

Robert Sachs

BOOKS

Winchester, UK
Washington, USA

JOHN HUNT PUBLISHING

First published by O-Books, 2020
O-Books is an imprint of John Hunt Publishing Ltd., 3 East St., Alresford,
Hampshire SO24 9EE, UK
office@jhpbooks.com
www.johnhuntpublishing.com
www.o-books.com

For distributor details and how to order please visit the 'Ordering' section on our website.

ISBN: 978 1 78904 438 6
978 1 78904 439 3 (ebook)
Library of Congress Control Number: 2019948225

A CIP catalogue record for this book is available from the British Library.

Design: Stuart Davies

UK: Printed and bound by CPI Group (UK) Ltd, Croydon, CR0 4YY
US: Printed and bound by Thomson-Shore, 7300 West Joy Road, Dexter, MI 48130

We operate a distinctive and ethical publishing philosophy in
all areas of our business, from our global network of authors to
production and worldwide distribution.

Contents

Dedication

There have been many people and influences in my life which have contributed to me becoming a better, more civil human and being.

First and foremost, I wish to thank my parents, Sherman and Thelma Sachs. They loved each other and they cared for their children as best they could in the face of the anti-Semitism that ravaged us as a family. Civilly righteous, they were honest, sometimes too candid, but never had the intent to harm.

There are the many Buddhist Masters and friends who have taught and supported me in a deep, fulfilling meditative practice and life – in particular H.H. 16th Karmapa, H.E. Kunzig Shamar Rinpoche, Ven. Chime Rinpoche, Ven. Trungpa Rinpoche, Ven. Khenpo Karthar Rinpoche, and my dear friend and teacher, Lama Ole Nydahl.

Over the last several years, I have benefitted greatly in my pursuit, membership, and studies in Freemasonry. Grand Masters of California, MW Russ Charvonia, M. David Perry, and John Heisner, WB Peter Champion, WB Robert Bettencourt, WB Christian Marano, WB Dave Chesebro, WB Chuck Dunning and WB Doug Russell of the Academy of Reflection – these Brothers I single out among many others whose friendship and mentorship I cherish.

Special thanks to Michael Mann and the publishing house of John Hunt – thank-you in having confidence in this project.

And last, but always, my Beloved Melanie – for tolerating the many times I have gone down the rabbit hole to ponder and write. You are precious and a model of civility traversing the many roads and adventures we have traveled together along the way. Hand in hand, let's continue to love and serve.

Introduction

In the mid-twentieth century, a well-known mystic from the East was asked by a journalist what he thought of what he had seen thus far of Western civilization.

Gandhi's response: "I think it would be a good idea."

His response was in no way a put-down; that somehow his Indian culture was superior or more civilized. For, being also a great humanitarian, Gandhi knew all too well the ubiquitous follies and failings of human endeavors – the greed, corruption, political wranglings and so forth of his own and many other nations of the world throughout history. As a well-respected man of spirit, he knew, practiced, and sought to teach as many people as he came into contact with what he prayed would contribute to societies and nations founded upon and earnestly trying to bring out the best in each of its citizens. Like all holy men, his hope was to contribute to the creation of nations, spurred on by inspired, compassionate leaders to build a peaceful, sustainable, and civil world dedicated to the eradication of the sickness, poverty, and warfare which have too often dominated the human narrative on this planet, everywhere and in all times.

The beacon of a shining light on the hill, a nation founded on such ideals is not new. Within our own Western culture, principles of the Enlightenment of the eighteenth century – liberty, equality, and fraternity – stirred the vision of America's founding brothers and sisters. Yet their introduction to the American continent did not reflect these values. Indeed, there were many who came to these shores in search of a better life, one free especially from the religious persecution they had endured in their European homelands. But the desire of these immigrants was marked by their own beliefs that the tribal cultures they met, already well established on this continent, were inferior and heathen. Blinded by the bias of their worldview that declared them superior in faith and culture, some and probably most hoped to peacefully move in, eventually show their neighbors the errors of their ways or just be left alone. But there were also those immigrants who felt divinely justified to commit heinous and murderous actions to establish their own dominance over the land, the people, and all its resources. There were the many discoverers, entrepreneurs, and people whose focus was more on their own wealth, power, and self-aggrandizement in a brand-new land. They chose to use their superior firepower and/or beliefs in their "god-given" right to take what they could and obliterate those who stood in their way to do so if they were not willing to comply with this "divine" or "destined" plan.

This is NOT a unique story of expansion and dominance, of kingdom building. The Persians, the Greeks, the Romans, the Turks, the Chinese, the Indians, the Mongolians, the Russians, the Spanish, the Germans, the Japanese – East and West have participated in their own forms of ethnic cleansing, manifest destiny, inquisitions, empire building – all justified politically or ecclesiastically, or both.

The Hurdy Gurdy Man

In the late 1960s the Scottish psychedelic singer and songwriter Donovan wrote…

Histories of ages past
Unenlightened shadows cast
Down through all eternity
The crying of humanity

'Tis then when the Hurdy Gurdy Man
Comes singing songs of love
Then when the Hurdy Gurdy Man
Comes singing songs of love

Although my dire diatribe decries humanity's inhumanity and incivility to the "others" of humanity, there has always been a nobler, kinder side that has even wielded its head during times of persecution, domination, and conflagration.

While the thirst for power and riches blinded (and continues to blind) rulers, generals, and the privileged who sought more for just being privileged, we see symbols and gestures of parlay, peace, truce, and surrender; white flags, olive branches, smoke signals, back-door diplomatic channels. Even though these means may have not been employed in good faith, they bespeak a common understanding that in order for peace or equilibrium to be reestablished, **civility** is a powerful tool when passions and stakes are high.

From stories of the battlefields in history, I am reminded of the Christmas truce between Allied forces and the Germans in WWI, where soldiers came out of their foxholes and extended to each other gifts and Christmas greetings. A little known fact from Freemasonry was that during America's War for Independence, when British forces captured an American town previously held by Revolutionary forces, they would not destroy the town's Masonic Lodge, but rather, took the charter out of the building and delivered it to the retreating Revolutionary force Masons, who reciprocated when the tables were reversed. In a more ancient tradition from the East, warriors were trained that when they had mortally wounded a foe, that they should sit down, hold the foe's head in their lap, comfort them and sing prayers for a better rebirth until they passed.

Despite the influence of our worst inclinations individually and collectively, love, compassion, and gestures and actions of civility continually remind us that we are capable of and can always do better.

At some point and hopefully before even darker times, we hear "the crying of humanity."

The Age of Enlightenment

What distinguishes the 1700s during the "Age of Enlightenment" is perhaps that there was a greater collective of thinkers, East and West, and beyond the enclaves of the parochial religious, where the separation between the sacred and mundane was not so fixed and who believed that it was possible "to create a more perfect union." Despite the savagery, barbarity, and hubris of our ancestors, even our neighbors, it was possible to actualize and really implement our better instincts, rooted in the love and compassion espoused by those to whom we turned for solace and guidance. This dream was built upon the imperfections of our collective past, an awareness and acknowledgement of the legacy of those who demonstrated civility and nobility of character, with the goal to create that which would elevate and truly express civilization at its finest.

Born into this time in history, George Washington – recognized not only as the most exalted "father" of the American nation, the first President of the United States, but also a man highly regarded by leaders around the globe – was strongly influenced by the Age of Enlightenment. In a time when science and industry was expanding amid the ravages of the Middle Ages and continuous war and intrigue amongst factions of Christendom, "free" thinkers were embracing a re-imagining of their faiths, seeing a God that was not only transcendent, but also imminent in all things, including man. Deists and others like them were no longer looking for absolution from their human tendencies or a mere exoteric adherence to moral and ethical prescriptions in order to be civil and civilized. They saw each and every one of us as playing the essential role in learning ways to understand and transform our own behaviors from within. One example is the movement of Freemasonry, established as a fraternity in 1717 in England, founded on the tenets of brotherly love, relief, and truth, demanding of its members to study that which circumscribed our earthly desires in order to accomplish these noble intents.

In his *1776*, historian and author David McCullough tells how Washington who, though from landed gentry in Virginia, did not receive the benefit of more than eight years of formal education. Washington, himself, considered this a disadvantage, making him self-conscious in the presence of those whom he considered as more learned or of an elevated status in the society of the time. A man of great stature and bearing – being six foot two inches in a time when the average man was a clear six to ten inches shorter – he was used to hard work and had a practical knowledge of the land, learned the ways of military discipline, distinguished himself in that arena while also becoming a Freemason, himself, at the age of 20.[1] His military career and the moral and ethical lessons and leadership training in Freemasonry would more than compensate for a lack of knowledge in teaching him how to present himself with the dignity and civility he saw so essential to social and personal harmony. We know that these latter points, dignity and civility, were so essential to his training and resulting character from an early age. One of the few examples we have of writings penned by Washington is a little booklet he wrote as a young man, known as *Rules of Civility & Decent Behavior in Company and Conversation*.

As early as the second century BCE, traders and adventurers were travelling the Silk Road, which connected the Orient to the Mediterranean. Thus, there would have been an awareness of Buddhism and the cultures that ascribed to its tenets. The famous Marco Polo records his encounters and reflections on the Tibetan masters he met and observed while visiting the Chinese Imperial Court. Thus the teachings of the Buddha would have been known to thinkers, philosophers, and spiritual aspirants of Europe during the Age of Enlightenment in the eighteenth century. How these teachings, with their emphasis on personal growth, responsibility, enlightenment, and altruistic action to the benefit of others may have influenced this Age of Enlightenment has no doubt been investigated. But, in talking about how to interpret *Perfecting the Lessons of a President by Applying the Wisdom of a Buddha*, I wish to focus on the person and circumstance of the historical Buddha, Sakyamuni, who lived nearly twenty-two centuries earlier.

Sakyamuni, whose birth name was Siddhartha Gautama, had a different background and training. Born to be a king, his education was the finest in its day, and he learned the ways of power and leadership that he was presumed to deploy when it was his time. But, after a series of life-changing events and using his own power of reasoning, he concluded that his life's purpose was not to take on the throne after his father, but rather, pursue a life more focused on spiritual, rather than worldly rewards.

I say "spiritual" rather than "religious" because the teachings he gave and would be known as the *dharma* (translated: the way things are) flew in the face of the Hindu views and caste system that dominated the Indian subcontinent. Like Western Age of Enlightenment thinkers who saw the ravages of the Middle Ages, the Crusades, and so forth, Siddhartha Gautama knew of the strife, intrigues, and even wars waged in the name of or for religion throughout India. But rather than taking sides, he stepped back and took a more dispassionate approach. His conclusion was that if God and the laws of God are objective truths and people are killing each other over the interpretation given, then the problem is not with God or God's laws, but rather in the minds of humans who have their own subjective biases as to who God is and what he/she means. Thus, what we need to do is examine how we think, how we come to the conclusions that we do. Thus the dharma of the Buddha is really a mind science much more than it is a religion. And the goal of these teachings by he who would be known as the Buddha

Sakyamuni was to transform our worst tendencies to awaken to our inherent goodness and become more peaceful and "civil" to each other. One could argue that the path the Buddha lays out **is** exemplified in the world as "The Path of Civility."

The Buddha never cloistered himself or those who followed him away from society. Indeed there were retreats in remote, peaceful areas to support ongoing, intense meditations and contemplations. But, for the most part, many of the communities he formed were close to urban centers, where even the layperson could come to learn to meditate, learn how to calm down, and learn to be a better citizen. But, this did not mean that the spiritual communities or its members around the Buddha were the models of such. Being well educated and savvy to the ways of the world of men, he could see that the religious life had every bit as much political wrangling as the royal court. Thus, he allowed his transcendent eye to bring a focus on social and communal life, be it secular or religious. And, the conversations and recommendations he makes regarding speech, conduct, and actions have stood the test of time. Hence it is that the wisdom shared in teachings known as sutras applies as much to modern secular life as it did to the religious sects and communities of antiquity.

In essence, both Washington and the Buddha shared an understanding of social and communal life and the necessity for Civility to be an important civilizing feature.

Civility as a Path and the Layout of this Book

The Buddha and the President were aware of their social and political status. And although one would pursue a religious life while the other a life of public service, both had a fundamental awareness of the social nature of humanity, and that **civility** was essential if human transactions were to bring peace, harmony, and freedom from the many vicissitudes of mortal life. They were also acutely aware that the demonstration and fruition of civility in the world of men and women only becomes possible through the training, discipline, and mindful awareness that hones the skills and attributes we have been gifted as humans.

So, how does one create a Path of Civility? That is the purpose of this book.

I shall first start with some working definitions, beginning with civility, passion, and compassion; that in order for civility to become a reality, we need to transform our passions into compassion. In Chapter Two, I shall present concepts from the teachings of the Buddha that will be the basis for laying out the Path. I shall delineate levels of compassion and how to succeed in each through the application of what I have called The Five Steps of Wise Action. Chapter Three will focus on what the Buddha had to say about speech and conversing with greater awareness and civility. Useful "Mind Training" slogans are the focus of Chapter Four. In this chapter, I shall also provide one of the most potent Buddhist meditations for transforming negative states of mind and conflict with others. Chapter Five is devoted to Washington's "Rules of Civility." In these last three chapters, after each quote, slogan, or rule, I shall add some commentary in order to place each in the context of our modern times and the many challenges we face when trying to live in peace with civility in a world in search of both.

Chapter One

Civility, Passion, and Compassion

Civility is rooted in an altruistic spirit, founded on an understanding that we are *basically good* and that we best grow and succeed through cooperation.

Such a perspective seems an obvious feature in the establishment of a civilized society. But, as we see in the world that such a perspective appears rare, we need to get more basic with our definitions to get to this place.

First of all, what does it mean to be "civil"?

The online definition refers to two primary qualities – courteous and polite. Other words used are respectful, gallant, and well-mannered which then leads to the notion of someone being well-bred. Thus, to be civil is not necessarily an innate characteristic of being human, but something that must be taught.

Note that in this definition and its synonyms, words such as affection, like, love, harmony or being harmonious, or agreement are not used, even implied. Thus to be "civil" does not mean that one has to have affection for, be in agreement with, feel harmonious towards another with whom you are engaged.

If you put this notion as basically defined within the context of a "civilization," then it can be said that what helps a civilization hold together is that there is an attempt to maintain an equilibrium where different cultures, nations, opinions may or may not be in harmony, but venture to live by a code where courtesy and consideration are seen as the first and most basic modes of behavior. In this light, civility, is the glue and balm that can lead to harmony, and the way to conflict resolution should such arise which, in the realm of human activity, seems almost inevitable.

And yet, the way in which I define civility at the outset of this chapter makes it almost seem that to be civil as described should be so natural, so easy, so uplifting. In truth, it is. But, for this to be the case, we need to understand and cultivate our *basic goodness* – a term which now needs defining.

Basic Goodness

The phrase *basically good* was coined by the Tibetan Buddhist teacher, Venerable Chögyam Trungpa Rinpoche. It rests on the Buddhist principle that each of us possesses the capacities and abilities to awaken to our full human potential, our *Buddha nature*. This basic goodness demonstrates itself naturally in a spirit of intrinsic altruism; a loving care for others. Altruism as an intrinsic human quality may be viewed with skepticism as we witness the results of avarice, greed, self-centered, and me-first behavior every day, everywhere. But, we also observe that nothing brings us greater lasting pleasure or happiness than when we see others whom we love happy, satisfied, content, safe, secure, and so forth. Furthermore, the happiness we experience in seeing others happy, etc. seems more lasting than the pleasure or happiness we have when it is just about us or our self-centered desires.

The Three Poisons

That we do not demonstrate our Buddha nature or basic goodness and act in the spirit of altruism in our daily lives is not that we don't possess it or the result of sin as we commonly think in the West. Buddhas teach that we do not fully manifest this inherent goodness because of what are identified as Three Poisons of our mind and emotions: namely *Ignorance, Attachment, and Aggression*. Basically, we do not understand fully the world around us. We get attached to a limited and limiting point of view. And we get aggressive or defensive in holding to that view. If we reflect on our experience and are honest with ourselves, each one of us can identify and see these poisons at work in our lives.

The most essential purpose of contemplation and meditation in the Buddhist sense is to transform these Three Poisons into their actual awakened states: an awareness of our full potentials rooted in an open mind and great joy. Known best as the *unlimited mind, spontaneous joy, and unlimited potential* (aka *rainbow body*) these are the qualities exemplified in a truly awakened being, or Buddha.

When we are not educated or trained to see the world holistically, the world is smaller and becomes based on our own untrained mind, with its biases and blind spots. By definition and almost inevitably, our view becomes more self-referencing and centered. This does not mean that what we think or how we view is inherently bad. But, more than likely, as the world around us challenges our view, our first reaction becomes initially to recoil out of self-protection. This act of contraction to a safer distance then becomes the springboard from where we can either open up to a newer view, or go on the attack. If the world we have been constructing has been well serving us, then more than likely, we go on the attack. The civility or peaceful façade we may have had when everything was going our way gives way.

Beings of Passion

The philosophical view of the Buddha's teachings explains that the Three Poisons are potentially intertwined with another factor of our lives. Our human existence, though it possesses – as all existences of otherworldly beings do – basic goodness, is dominated and ruled by passion.

PASSION – most of us agree – is something we like to have in our lives; towards our partners, our children, our work or what we are "Called" to do, for life itself... But, if passion is not kept within due bounds, if it runs amuck under the influence of the Three Poisons, then the resulting self-centered perspective leads to passion becoming too intense, too heated. The world not going our way or not going our way as well as we want it to go, our focus shrinks, our survival instincts get activated, and it would seem that our civilized demeanor takes a back seat. That is, as our passions go up, our civility goes down!

Our passion, under the sway of the Three Poisons, creates not only our own personal dramas, but is at the core of the avarice and greed that lead to large-scale, global issues, simply expressed in the three greatest plagues of humanity: sickness, poverty, and warfare.

These three plagues have been with humanity since time immemorial. Yet, the historical Buddha, Sakyamuni, pointed to a future time, when the intensity of all these would come to a crescendo in a future "dark age." According to His prediction and the time frame he specified, we *are* in that Dark Age. A Dark Age is not about a world that is no longer viable being the ultimate threat, but rather the clouds in our own minds that prevent us from engaging each other with civility and respect in order to work together to solve the problems that inevitably are put before any species living on a planet with limited resources needing to be managed sustainably for the benefit of all.

Whilst the problems mentioned are age-old, there are, to my mind, some barriers to the civility needed to solve the world's plagues that are unique to our times.

A Survival State of Mind

There are many in the world who exist on subsistence or less, and thus, securing food, avoiding dangerous predators, animal or human, and staying as healthy as possible is as good as it gets. The politics of the day, wars in other lands, and environmental degradation and collapse may be impacting them. But, when your needs are so immediate, what's causing your lack seems irrelevant to having some bread and feeling safe in the moment.

There is a body of evidence that points to the fact that many of the world's problems are better understood and that caring people feeling their *basic goodness* are working to eradicate them.

But, as a more inclusive perspective on our interconnectedness emerges, there are those more entrapped by their own self-centeredness. Seeing their privilege and power under attack, these individuals and groups are fostering perspectives of nationalism, xenophobia, and other forms of exclusivism. Thus, in keeping with the oriental philosophical standpoint in which it is said, "What has a front has a back. The bigger the front, the bigger the back," the light of awareness is being challenged by the darkness of myopia and its resulting fear.

Although this polarity of view is nothing new, the weaponry and potential to inflict tactical or overall annihilation has never been greater.

Add to this climate change.

We are on a planet spinning through space, and as such, there are inevitable changes that will occur as continents drift, split, and change with cosmic influences. These are unavoidable. But then, there are the choices we make to devastate ecosystems, suck the oil out of the ground, and burn fossil fuels – all of which exacerbate the inevitable. It's like jumping out of a plane with a bag of rocks on your back rather than a parachute.

Thus, along with our usual sickness, poverty, and warfare is the very real existential threat to our overall existence as a species.

With increased human drama and the passion to survive still under the influence of the Three Poisons, our ability to sit down with each other and figure out what best we can do is hampered by the emotions of sadness, anger, anxiety, depression and fear. That this is a truth of modern life is exemplified in our inability to modulate or regulate our moods without some kind of prescribed or recreational substance. True civility does not really exist in an "It's all good, man" blather or dialogue under the influence of Xanax, marijuana, OxyContin, or a very nice pinot noir.

Digital Communication

Our passion to connect has led us to create the frequency and speed we celebrate in digital communication and which leads to its opposite. The endless and perpetual micro-messages we receive at every juncture of thought create more drama and confusion.

A simple example on a personal level...

You are upset with someone. In the past, you would write a letter, which you would then fold, put in an envelope, address, stamp, and then walk to the mailbox and post. And, every step of the way, you may have second thoughts, even get to the mailbox, decide not to put the envelope in the box, or tear it up. Somehow, in the process of just writing, you were able to get out your venom, decompress a bit, and think of a more civil option to solve the matter.

But, with e-mail or texting, rather than have the time to mechanically put together a response to mail, you can digitally spew your venom then and there. Rather than having a moment of pause, perhaps a moment of your *basic goodness* winning the day, the venom of the moment is already doing its damage and a similar knee-jerk response is more than likely already on its way back to you.

This is a personal example. Maybe you have done this via Instagram, Snapchat, a text, or e-mail. But, you could have also gone to Facebook, Twitter and taken your personal squabble to a whole new level of backlash and retort.

Now, let's take a 24-hour news cycle.

Fox, CNN, MSNBC, NBC, CBS, etc... all awaiting a tweet, the newest he said/she said quips, getting endless minute-by-minute updates, creating "breaking news," breaking news that is almost as instantly momentous as breaking wind. (This last comment may seem facetious, but it is interesting to note that the Buddha predicted this to be a time when the winds of physical existence would be excessive, resulting in chronic diseases, mental illness, and mental confusion creating more conflict. In the body, the winds referred to actually create gas and constipation.)

And so we live in a time when we do not honor the blessings of time. In the speed of immediate feedback and response, there is no pause, and as such, no patience. Everything becomes pressured, and thus to know what is and what is not of consequence becomes harder and harder to discern.

The Speed of Life

In an interview I did with the Ven. Tarthang Tulku Rinpoche for my book *The Wisdom of the Buddhist Masters: Common and Uncommon Sense*, he said that beyond what each of us experience as the passage of time feeling faster as we get older, there actually was a speeding up of time that has a physical truth and, with it, numerous discernable effects. Seeing this speeding up of our reality and witnessing the effects of greed and power in human societies and on the planet overall, he was not optimistic that we would be able to reverse course for many of the human and environmental catastrophes in which we are a part even as of today.

In our inattentiveness to our better instincts and allowing the Three Poisons to steer our passionate nature towards a self-centered self-destruction, it would seem that a call to civility is the least of our problems, and quite possibly beyond overdue and not even worth bothering with.

Although we have many wise teachers and teachings to help steer us in a better direction, it seems that disaster has always been our best teacher. Then, and only then, our better instincts and, with it, our basic goodness emerge, and we realize that cooperation is the best approach to work on a course correction. In which case, civility becomes a vital tool in getting us all to the table, to listen to each other, and act accordingly. In this regard, civility is a KEY ingredient and absolutely worthy of our attention.

Passion, Love, and Compassion

If we are beings of passion, can passion really be the enemy of civility? Or, do we need to train ourselves to harness our passions and – as we have a few times repeated earlier – keep them within due bounds? Does this mean we are restraining or repressing our passions? Or, are we transforming them into something greater, where passion's warmth and joy is wedded to our basic goodness?

In transforming through taming and working "with" our passion and passions we bring out our best as a species. I emphasize the word "with" because "with passion" is none other than COMPASSION; that to passion, we add something. That something, our basic goodness, which when melded to passion yields the most potent force on our planet: LOVE. When we learn to access our basic goodness passionately and activate the love that gives heart to our altruistic spirit, we are living a COMPASSIONATE life. Furthermore, if we hold to our earlier definition of civility, then we see that civility and compassion go hand in glove; that with compassion, our words and actions bear the mark of civility as the best way to inspire and work with others to achieve our most cherished dream of a peaceful and possibility-rich world in which to thrive.

The next chapter will look more closely at COMPASSION, its four faces and how civility is demonstrated in its various applications.

Chapter Two

Wisdom, Compassion, and Civil Action

Civility, viewed from the perspective I have laid out thus far, implicitly arises and is experienced by others and us when we come to more fully recognize our inseparability and interdependence with all life as exemplified in compassionate expression and action.

Defining and delineating types of compassion is the primary focus of this chapter. But, before exploring compassion more fully, let us first examine the qualities or characteristics we might observe in civility thus defined.

Although decorum and propriety are often cited as characteristics, I shall, for this discussion, break them down further, adding some additional and clarifying characteristics. There are four altogether: presence, time, timing and tone. To these, I shall also introduce the Buddhist behavioral qualities known as the Six Perfections.

Presence and the Six Perfections

Presence is more than just decorum. Decorum covers how you present yourself; your appearance, demeanor, and your manner. In Washington's "Rules of Civility," these qualities are explored extensively, and with my commentaries, are the final chapter of this work. The Buddha's Six Perfections add to this concise behaviors to be perfected and exemplified by those engaging in civil discourse and acts of civility.

The Six Perfections (Sanskrit: *Paramitas*) are considered to be what distinguishes the manner and actions of an enlightened being from those of us still embroiled in emotional turmoil and conflict. Furthermore, they are those qualities which we should aspire to perfect if we wish to become enlightened ourselves.

These Six Perfections are: Generosity, Kindness, Patience, Discipline, Stillness (i.e. Meditative Awareness), and Wisdom.

A **Generous spirit** is one that exhibits openness and a willingness to share freely. This does not mean that one disregards history or goes into a situation with rose-colored glasses. Rather, one enters into an interaction with a sense of – what Freemasons would call – "being on the level." In the world of human interaction there are always distinctions that have to do with rank, position, authority, and so forth. But, these distinctions should not be viewed as an absolute pecking order where some are really higher than you while others are below you. Such a view will make social interaction contrived and stifling. But, if we see that we are all on the level in the eyes of Creation and the Divine however we define it, then it is possible to "render unto Caesar what is Caesar's," while engaging anyone and everyone in a manner which demonstrates a willingness to be open.

Kindness does not mean that you are a soft pushover. It means you act without guile or a twist to make things go to your advantage to the disadvantage of the other simply because you want to win or be on top. You are straightforward in a way that allows for a transaction to feel two-way or serve the greatest number in the most beneficial way possible.

Being **Patient** in our action will be discussed with Propriety. Here, I look at an internal quality, which is an understanding of the time it takes for our mind and habits to transform. How often do we see our own history repeating itself, where what we thought were habits or actions we had changed, once again emerge in a new or different circumstance? We then get down on ourselves, get disappointed, and then this self-denigration skews our behavior towards others. In *patiently* tending to our own awakening, when our confusion dawns as wisdom, we demonstrate a mercy towards ourselves, which will well serve us when we are trying to encourage a change of mind or action in others.

The Tibetan word for **Discipline** (*tsul trim*) also means *joy*. These two may seem on opposite ends of a spectrum. However, if we know what to do and how to do it well in any given circumstance, there is less stress and more ease in what happens. Rather than observing heaviness and intensity, we observe a lightness to the situation. Thus discipline in speech, knowing what to say, how to deliver it so that your message comes across most effectively, is a skill worth cultivating. This does not mean that every word needs to be memorized to the point of seeming wholly contrived. But, to have contemplated and decided what is and what is not of use to get your point across creates the greatest likelihood that what you are trying to get across *is* what gets across. Then, even if what transpires involves extemporaneous comments, because you have parried down what needs to be said in a disciplined fashion, the commentary that follows will likely be more to the point and delivered likewise. The Ven. Trungpa Rinpoche used to talk about "good head and shoulders." This is about a quality of uprightness, of dignity, a by-product of discipline.

Stillness or Meditative Awareness invites an open and clear mind. To not have your internal dialogue chatting away while you are trying to pay attention and listen reduces the likelihood of you interrupting or adding commentary that is more about you than about the transaction you are trying to be engaged in. This requires training. Such training may be the various meditations in both Eastern and Western traditions. Such awareness may also be developed by actively spending time in nature. A demeanor, which exhibits this quality, also encourages a stillness in the people and circumstance one is engaged with. Tibetan Buddhist teachers speak of "taming" a situation in this manner.

Finally, there is **Wisdom**. Although we all have the Awakening potential to be wise, all the qualities mentioned above, practiced well over time, will yield this perfection. Such wisdom commands respect implicitly and almost naturally. And when this does not happen, one does need all the qualities of generosity, kindness, patience, discipline, and stillness to encourage the greatest wisdom to be the informing data, attitudes, and call for action in the engagement.

Buddhist teachers encourage us to develop all of these qualities. However, we may find that some of these qualities are hard for us to personify, while others seem more natural to whom we are. For example, perhaps you are a very kind person, but not very patient. A Buddhist master would tell you to work on your strengths rather than fret about your weaknesses. With this in mind, if you keep strengthening your kindness, more than likely patience will begin to grow in you as a result.

Time and Timing

Propriety is closely linked to decorum. In fact, many of the traits I have discussed above with respect to presence would also fall under the definition of propriety. However, I would like to focus on those attributes more connected to time and timing, namely correctness, decency, and good manners.

Time is different than timing in that it is more global than specific. Ecclesiastes 3:1-8 says,

To every thing there is a season,
and a time to every purpose under the heaven.

Sometimes we want to see change. And, it may even be that in the history of civilizations, time for important changes were overdue, and what was not addressed on time, led to great demise – at least from our limited perspective. In the face of climate change and shift, our inattention to the needs to adjust and adapt may, indeed, be now too late. And, we shall have a time in which we shall need to address what comes next.

But, even if we look at issues less cataclysmic, we see that wise individuals and leaders have noted a particular issue or issues that could not be changed in the climate of the day, but needed further time and change of heart and circumstances for the changes needed to be introduced or acted upon. In the case of the United States, slavery was one of those issues. And even when it was finally addressed, the Civil War that resulted did not destroy the country entirely as it might have at the nation's inception, but had devastating effects that we are still working out to this day. Was there a better time to effect such change? Or was it that the lancing of this boil on the American scene and psyche had finally reached a critical point and could be ignored no longer?

Thus, when addressing greater or lesser issues, to choose the best time to bring a matter up and deal with it implies correctness in understanding the situation. In this context, the next aspect of time is then Timing. Here, we can look at when parties will be most receptive. Decency and good manners come into the equation at this point. The calculation of these two implies also that there is some *sensitivity* to the situation. To have cultivated the stillness and patience of the Six Perfections explained above is most useful in cultivating this.

Tone, Morality, and the Four Levels of Compassion

What is a civil tone? Is it always sweet and soft? Is it always gentle?

Sadly, I think that many people define civility as weak or affected. Civility is then that tone one has when the matters are not pressing, where one can act as if at a tea party – unless one thinks of Boston...

In the spirit of basic goodness and rooted in altruism, where we are trying to come up with the best inclusive, positive solution to any matter, morality needs to be a factor. In fact, what I contend is that morality is that dimension which adds the passion to act compassionately. Without this dimension, civility becomes a tone of placation.

Of course, morality has both unconditional and conditional dimensions. In Buddhism, many meditations consider or literally begin with what are known as the Four Limitless Meditations.

May all beings have happiness and the causes of happiness.
May all beings be free from sorrow and the causes of sorrow.
May all beings never be separated from the great happiness that is beyond sorrow.
May all beings dwell in great equanimity, free from passion, aggression, and prejudice.

Simply put, we want to live a life informed by our basic goodness, help ourselves and others to be less swayed by the Three Poisons, and treat everyone fairly and impartially. A good friend and metaphysician, Geoffrey Bullington, simplifies this into an intentional phrase he uses in all of his actions and transactions with others:

For the goodness of all concerned.

If we hold to this moral perspective in the words and actions we do, then the Four Compassionate acts become truly effective with an authority that demonstrates true human caring.

Skillful Means and Wisdom

In its basic philosophy and all its meditation methods, Buddhism, like all wisdom traditions around the globe, identifies archetypal male and female principles. The male principle has to do with what is known as *skillful means*; in a word and more specifically, compassion. The female principle has to do with *wisdom*. If skillful means or compassion is not informed by wisdom, then the action will not really be all that skillful and will tend towards dogmatic responses, as in fascism. If wisdom is not wedded to skillful means or compassion, then it is for naught. It goes nowhere and leads to nothing. Thus, the two together, like yin and yang, yab and yum, Shiva and Shakti, Apollo and Athena, bring balance and skill in all actions and responses.

As wisdom must inform action, let us break down the perfection of wisdom as mentioned above into distinct stages.

The Five Steps to Wise Action

How do we learn to act with skill, with compassion, to accomplish what we aspire for ourselves and in this world in the most civil way?

Although Wisdom is one of the Perfections mentioned earlier, it in itself can be subdivided into mental processes we need to go through in order to go from wise perception to wise action. These processes are all classified as wisdoms, which, when seen collectively, create sensible and progressive action steps to know how to employ or what level of compassion to use. Note that the discussion of the Five Wisdoms in Buddhism usually includes more theoretical and theological discussion. I shall avoid these and focus on the actionable aspects of each, which can be applied in both sacred and mundane situations.

All Pervasive Wisdom – This first wisdom action step may be the hardest as it asks us to step back from the immediacy of the situation or at least be able to keep our passions from leading us to a rush to judgment. If we are able to step back, to see a bigger picture and place the situation into a larger perspective, we then create more of an opportunity to think out of or beyond the box we may otherwise be mentally and emotionally trapped in. Succinctly, the action step is: **Step back.**

Discriminating Wisdom – By stepping back and getting a clearer picture, we encourage our ability to judge impartially, but with discernment. Based on a wider perspective, we are not looking at "the truth," per se. Relative reality and truth are, at best, very slippery bedfellows. There are always so many sides and interpretations to any situation. And so, we discern as best we can and give an "honest" assessment. Honesty means we are coming from a place of integrity within ourselves. Honesty allows us to change our minds if more information comes to light. We may not always know "the truth," but we can always be honest. Thus, the action step here is: **Assess.**

Mirror-like Wisdom – This wisdom is reminiscent of our modern psychological understanding of projection, that what we see in the world is a mirror reflection of our state of mind. (What is fascinating is that modern neuroscience has identified Mirror Neurons, which are said to reside behind our hearts and that the information from these neurons goes up to our brain. Furthermore, there are more signals going from the heart to the brain than vice versa. And so, Japanese Buddhism speaks of the "heart-mind." It is also fascinating to reflect that this wisdom known as "mirror-like" predates our current knowledge of mirror neurons by centuries.) What is called on here is for us to understand the direct impact on us personally of what we have honestly assessed. If we start there, we stand a better chance of knowing how our words or actions that follow will affect others. The action step is: **Reflect.**

Wisdom of Equanimity – This wisdom demands that we confront within ourselves any bigotry that sees any person or being to be ultimately superior or inferior to ourselves. Freemasonry, as a tradition of philanthropy and secular enlightenment, speaks of "being on the level." Without understanding that we are all "equal in the eyes of God," true, heartfelt empathic communication and civility-based action is not possible. The Yiddish word here is to be a "mensch." Not seeing or acting as being higher or lower than those whom we engage, we overcome prejudice and invite a reciprocal response. Whether the response we get is indeed reciprocal is another matter. But, the point in demonstrating civility here is that we engage in such a spirit. Engaging another "on the level," another important dimension of this wisdom is that *we do not engage in character assassination*. What we should be addressing are issues and actions. Thus, the action step here is: **Engage.**

All Accomplishing Wisdom – Being able to step back, assess, reflect, and properly engage, we now have the sufficient knowledge that we need to learn, summon and martial our energy wisely and apply it where, when, and how it is most effective. We step into action forthrightly. The action step here is: **Enact.**

The first three of these wisdoms, all-pervasive, discriminating, and mirror-like, are more internal or mental. The last two, the wisdom of equanimity and all-accomplishing wisdom, are the connection we make with others and our action or words in the manifest world. The bridge between the internal and outer or external is at the level of **mirror-like wisdom**, associated in the East with what is called the heart chakra, the center of the heart-mind. Reflection therefore acts as the gate between our inner machinations of our experience and how we are to prepare ourselves for engagement and action in the world. It is then by the wisdom of equanimity that we make the main step of social engagement. Thus, the **wisdom of equanimity** is the most social of all the wisdoms.

To summarize and succinctly state, in the Five Steps to Wise Action... we

1. **step back** – look at the big picture
2. **assess** – clearly discern what we are looking at
3. **reflect** on this knowledge, understand our part – making it personal, helping us to develop empathy
4. **engage** – initiate action based on mutual respect and intention of focusing on the good of all
5. **enact** – step into action forthrightly

The Four Levels of Compassion expounded

The Four Levels of Compassion are thus informed by the first three wisdoms and then manifest through the final two. It is at this point, therefore, that we need to fully explore each of the Levels or acts of compassion. In Buddhist philosophy, they are elucidated and enumerated in a particular order, from easy and peaceful to more challenging or confrontational. They are: pacifying, enriching, magnetizing, and destroying or wrathful. In the descriptions that follow, I shall be focusing mostly on action rather than the use of words or speech as the vehicle of tone. Although the tone of engagement through conversing is discussed here, civility in speech will be the general focus of the following chapter, "Proper Speech and Civil Dialogue." At the same time, I will note a *"reactive pattern"*: an action or response that can subvert the level of compassion being employed. These "reactive patterns" are to be noted in both actions and words.

Pacifying or Peaceful Compassion – In this situation, there is harmonious, empathic resonance amongst all proponents of a given direction/action. Conversations and actions feel like everyone is on the same page, or at least able to work with each other with the minimal of friction. The image is one of a team, and regardless of the part you play on that team, everyone is valued equally for their contribution. This is "the ideal" and often people want to project that this is actually the case. The language and actions taken are done all so pleasantly, thus the ideal of what it means to be civil. But, such civility is very conditional, perhaps fragile. Thus, there can be undermining shock or dismay when it is discovered that, somewhere down the line, unexpected or unanticipated subconscious agendas begin to surface. The larger picture or issue may seem to be seen by all as if in agreement. But, we must remember that "the devil is in the details," always. Because of the seeming simpatico, people become lazy and don't necessarily really engage the first three wisdoms thoroughly. This actually makes this form of compassion the hardest to practice skillfully because discernment seems unnecessary. Hence, the REACTIVE PATTERN to safeguard against: **Smugness (in-crowding).** *This reactive pattern is especially prevalent in organizations that feel they have a calling or mission – such as religious, political, or humanitarian enterprises.* **The tone of civility here is that of the Peacekeeper and Peace supporter.**

Enrichment Compassion – To get to a state of harmony in action, there needs to be further education. Thus, civility here is instructional, needing more reasoning, explanation, and a sense of empowering others – enriching them at various levels in order for them to get on board or be in alignment with what you want to achieve or express. The role teacher, mentor, or "a reliable source" is the civil tone you need to express and direct action from. **The tone of civility here is that of the Educator or Mentor.** The challenge and the REACTIVE PATTERN to safeguard against: **Condescension.** A useful phrase when this form of compassion is warranted: **"Have you considered...?"**

Magnetizing Compassion – Here, one meets with resistance, indifference, views more rooted in the Three Poisons. To influence this situation, the power of persuasion, the use of charisma, a more emotional/feeling-based approach becomes necessary to rally support for the desired direction/action/outcome. How can we attract those we need for successful action away from the "dark side"? The focus of the conversation should be contrasting the **consequences** of unskillful action versus the **rewards** of skillful actions. To do this, while the presentation is more at an emotional or feeling level, the tone needs to be one of rationality; that one has carefully assessed the situation and wants to be informative for everyone's benefit. **The tone of civility here is that of the Statesman or Evocateur.** The REACTIVE PATTERN to safeguard against: **Manipulation (especially through inappropriate flattery, etc.).** A useful phrase: **"What are the pros and cons...?"**

Wrathful Compassion – Here, you are dealing with intractable people or a very difficult circumstance. Thus, confrontation or action to prevent action/decisions that are deemed harmful is considered necessary. It is always truly difficult to know if this is, in fact, the case. Hence, the three internal wisdoms need to be fully practiced. The Wisdom of Equanimity may be hard to practice in engagement as there is obvious conflict. Thus, one needs to be sure that no advantage is being taken or power employed just simply because you can do so. While the words or actions used may need to be stronger than you would normally use, perhaps even harsh, the use of this form of compassion must be rooted in love and humility. That this is the basis of the action taken will be seen in feelings of remorse or regret that actions of this nature needed to be enacted. If possible, to express this remorse or regret can be a necessary salve of civility in order for the party on the receiving end not to feel that you are merely acting in the REACTIVE PATTERN of **Vengeance or Revenge**. **The tone of civility here is that of the Protector.** Because this form of compassion and its civility has the potential of bearing the most heat of passion, staying focused on the issues rather than going after the personality or character of the person or persons can be more challenging. If one were to be rating civil discourse, probably any discourse that involves the degradation of another's character would be the lowest and most regrettable. But, then again, sometimes in social and political arenas humiliation may be a necessary component in confrontation and/or stopping harmful action. But, I would argue, that it would at some point yield backlash that has to be addressed with a deeper sense of remorse. A useful phrase: **"I regret to inform you..."**

Civil Disobedience

In the tempestuous climate of personal attack politics, xenophobia, and the global resurgence of tribalism under the moniker of "nationalism," civility has been maligned in books and articles, social media, and so forth. Seen only within the context of the first level of compassion, "pacifying or peaceful," to those who overtly protest or act in indignant response to the forces which seem oblivious or non-responsive to sickness, poverty, and warfare, civility is seen as a form of social control; a way of keeping the masses in line, compliant.

That civility can be expanded to include the expressions I have thus described is, therefore, unthinkable, revolutionary – not really in keeping with the way in which the conventional mind wishes to keep civility in the "play nice" box. In a recent Facebook tete-a-tete, I was called to defend my expanded view of civility and its place in social and cultural change and transformation. For civility to be only defined as an affect, a benign response clearly does not do the term justice or reveal the power it has when applying the Five Steps of Wise Action and a more appropriate, dynamic form of compassionate speech or action. This brings us to the topic of *civil disobedience*.

Civil Disobedience falls under the last category of compassion – wrathful. To explain this more fully, let us break this phrase down, first.

Obedience involves the following of rules, laws, someone, or something because they are expected to be followed, by those creating the rules, the laws, the pecking order or such, sometimes by those who think they should or feel compelled to do so, or both.

In this respect, there are three levels of obedience. First and foremost where there is the greatest power disparity is that of submission; where following the rule, the law, the ideology, the lord of the manor is not only expected, but there are proscribed consequences for not doing so. Then there is an obedience where the rational or justification for following such or being under the banner of an ideology, or leader, is that one sees merit or something of value in obedience to such. In this there is a subtle line between and sometimes a combination of submission with a willful abdication of personal responsibility. Although this may create social harmony and a general sense of pacifying-type civility, whenever there is a power differential or a deference based on social or cultural norms, things do change. Furthermore, rarely do those whose power or mandates, which have been legitimated by fitting the times, give up their advantage when change is needed for the general good. Thus abdication of personal responsibility can slide into unwilling submission. Finally, there is obedience that comes from a mutual, "on the level" understanding. Thus, like the *paramita* or perfection of discipline, there is actual joy and benefit that comes from adherence to such.

If the time and circumstance we find ourselves in is no longer one of mutual benefit, where obedience becomes coerced or demanding of submission, then the *civil* approach, that which speaks to our basic goodness, must lead us to **distance** ourselves from such adherence. As stated previously in different ways, civility is dependent upon being on the level, where there is mutuality – or at least respect – even when there is a social, cultural, or spiritual disparity to which people subscribe.

What is the consequence when your position is "I regret to inform you that..." when you do not comply with the norms or legitimated laws, edicts, or rulers of which or to whom you have been – up to this point – obedient? Consider Nelson Mandala – imprisoned. Ang San Suu Kyi – imprisoned. Martin Luther King – assassinated. Mohandas Gandhi – assassinated. In the disparity of power, denial or disregard of the civil rights or benefits that create for a more just society, it becomes inevitable that those challenging these structures or rules become vilified, become seen as dissidents, malcontents, even terrorists, regardless of whether their actions and words are peaceful or confrontational. Then again, when coercion and force are used to suppress these malcontents, at what point can we say that reciprocal force is not unwarranted? In this, I am reminded of the words of the late Tibetan Buddhist Master, the Thirteenth Kunzig Shamar Rinpoche, who spoke of the necessity to sometimes wage what he called a "white war."[2]

Does this mean, therefore, that if the underdog or the righteous side of a "white war" proves victorious over the short- or long-term, there will not be consequences? After all, we see that in the working of relative reality situations, there is always a variation of hell to pay. The champions we have highlighted above were eloquent, charismatic, and demonstrative of propriety in a straightforward way. Their actions and words did catalyze or at least contributed to significant cultural and societal change. But other than their own trials and tribulations, there were many in their ranks that likewise suffered similar fates. And the results sought remain works in progress. Consider "Black Lives Matter," the "Me Too" movement, the time it takes to root out greed, corruption, and power mongering. That is why, for the changes sought to become more real and lasting, there needs to be an awareness of those qualities or traits that can undermine, slow down, even subvert the course of basic goodness envisioned in the world: greed, self-righteousness, revenge, and so forth.

In the case of America, we know that George Washington was an ardent believer in and aspiring practitioner of civility. And, yet, he was also a soldier, a general, and eventually the President of a country he supported in disobedience to what he and others defined as a tyrannical regime. As we reference President George Washington, with all the flaws, omissions, and unintended consequences of the American Revolution, and acknowledging that the very formation of this country had its own bloody history of conquest and slavery, many contend as do I that there was a genuine attempt to envision a different future. The men and women, the Founding Mothers and Fathers of America, were striving for a "more perfect union." Otherwise, the provisions of the First and Second Amendments of the American Constitution would not have been the first and second principles upon which to form the United States; a nation that to this day is still aspiring to be a true democracy.

> **Amendment ONE:** "Congress shall make no law respecting an establishment of religion, or prohibiting the free exercise thereof; or abridging the freedom of speech, or of the press; or the right of the people peaceably to assemble, and to petition the government for a redress of grievances."

This Amendment embodies a civil way of engaging in promoting truth and seeking to express grievances to elicit dialogue and change. And, our first three forms of compassion, Peaceful, Enrichment, and Magnetizing, are the methodologies that can help in the processes of maintaining civility in the change process. It is important to note that Enriching Compassion dependent on education was a major feature of what the formers of America felt to be needed for "true" democracy to prevail and be sustainable. Thus we see Washington being a champion for primary school education and a general agreement that there needs to be an availability of classical education in order to build an informed, civil electorate.

> **Amendment TWO:** "A well regulated Militia, being necessary to the security of a free State, the right of the people to keep and bear Arms, shall not be infringed."

This Amendment is more in line with the final form of compassion – wrathful.

Thomas Jefferson once commented that any country that wished to promote freedom and democracy needed to have a periodic revolution in order to avoid the resurgence and the inevitable slide back into tyranny. For civil society to be maintained, there need to be watchdogs, the soldiers of wrathful compassion, to ensure that the principles and practices "of the people, for the people, and by the people," be safeguarded. Hence, a separation between church and state and the independent functioning of branches of government are fundamental. But, just in case those of legitimated authority or in ruling positions in representative government get too full of themselves, there are always the people – and their guns.

This aforementioned option is a last and regrettable resort. For civil disobedience in both normal or extraordinary forms (i.e. revolutions) to be carried out in the most civil way possible, due diligence should be made to temper the heat of rising passions by employing the Five Steps of Wise Action, the civility as exemplified in the first three forms of compassion, and then step forward into this wrathful expression with a clarity of mind and heart that especially guards itself against self-righteousness. For this latter expression, self-righteousness is the poison that makes one anesthetized to vengeful actions, which, inevitably, spawn the most heinous reactions. In the chapter on "Mind Training" there will be a further explication on this point.

There are many aspects of wisdom and levels of compassion, so civility demonstrates itself effectively in different guises, all rooted in the same basic goodness, all intended from the same altruistic outlook. A "one size fits all" civility cannot meet the challenges of all the different ways in which people act as individuals or groups when the Three Poisons fuel reactivity and division. The goal of this chapter has been to point to action steps and approaches that will make civility dynamic and effective. Civility thus demonstrates itself as an essential rather than merely affective tool for change.

Chapter Three

Proper Speech and Civil Dialogue

As presented in the Introduction, the historical Buddha, Sakyamuni, was not of priestly class, but that of worldly rulers. Like the landed gentry of Washington's birth, both men were born into an expectation that when it was their time, they would inherit the mantle to be rulers of men, of society, of the land of their respective mandates. And while one sought a religious life and path and the other was a fighter and leader for a more temporal freedom, liberation was on both of their minds.

Though choosing an inherently spiritual life, the Buddha's worldly background and the background of the many who sought his guidance was a world of the sickness, poverty, and warfare that has visited all ages. Like Washington who, in a future time, saw the need to support education and train men and women in order to establish a more enlightened, harmonious, hence civil society, so Sakyamuni gave not only profound teachings on the mind and its transformation, but also many teachings on what is necessary to create social and communal harmony. In *The Ecology of Oneness*, I comment that there is no more political organization than one founded on religion. Thus it is that the Buddha could see that just because men and women come together in religious communities, it does not mean that their habits rooted in the Three Poisons go away as if by magic. Pettiness, in-crowds, sectarian strife, anger, bigotry, jealousy, and other negative emotions and associations create a culture rooted in subconscious, unfulfilled wants and desires that too often override the lofty ideals being strived for. Thus it is that the Pali Canon, the essential body of scriptures adhered to by the Theravadin Buddhists of Southeast Asia as the "Word of the Buddha," addresses any number of problems and challenges to social and communal harmony.

In 2016, Bhikkhu Bodhi compiled and edited a book, entitled, *The Buddha's Teachings on Social and Communal Harmony: An Anthology of Discourses from the Pali Canon*. There are many talks given by the Buddha that would no doubt contribute to civility. However, as other sections of this book expound on various teachings of the Buddha I have received over the years, for the purpose of this chapter, the discourses I wish to focus on have to do with what He called "Proper Speech." To the quotes and commentary given by Bhikkhu Bodhi, I shall also make some further comments in relation to their relevance to civil dialogue.

The power of words and speech was well known to the Buddha, who commented that for people to come to a proper understanding or "right view" beyond through their own discipline and practice was through "the utterance of another." Such speech which has as its intention the enlightening of another(s) can come as the verbal utterances in any of the four levels of compassion as elucidated in the previous chapter. However, there are general qualities of "proper speech" as an expression of skillful means that are the focus of this chapter and can be at all levels.

The first of the Buddha's points on speech that Bhikkhu Bodhi references is "**Well-Spoken Speech.**" This is not about enunciation per se (something that George Washington's "Rules of Civility" emphasize to demonstrate how a young man of good breeding should speak), but rather that "well" here almost implies *healthy* speech; speech that is clearly said, is truthful, and essentially pleasant. Even in the fourth level of compassion, where wrathfulness is required, it is still possible to fulfill these prerequisites.

In a series of stanzas from the Anguttara Nikaya, the Buddha provides general guidelines of "Well-Spoken Speech" with respect to speeches, discussions, debates, and so forth which encapsulate the points regarding conversing in "The Rules of Civility" as written down by George Washington. As translated by Bhikkhu Bodhi:

Those who speak with quarrelsome intent,
settled in their opinions, swollen with pride,
ignoble, having assailed virtues,
look for openings to attack one another.

They mutually delight when their opponent
speaks badly and makes a mistake,
they rejoice in his bewilderment and defeat;
but noble ones don't engage in such talk.

If a wise person wants to talk,
having known the time is right,
without quarrelsomeness or pride,
the sagely person should utter
the speech that the noble ones practice,
which is connected with the Dhamma and meaning.

Not being insolent or aggressive,
with a mind not elated,
on the basis of right knowledge.
He should approve of what is well expressed
but should not attack what is badly stated.

He should not train in fault finding
nor seize on the other's mistakes;
he should not overwhelm and crush his opponent,
nor speak mendacious words.
Truly, a discussion among the good
Is for the sake of knowledge and confidence.

Such is the way the noble discuss things;
this is the discussion of the noble ones.
Having understood this, the wise person
should not swell up but should discuss things.
(AN 3:67)[3]

The notion of "nobles" in the context of the Buddha's words refers to recognized spiritual teachers. However, within the spiritual or secular worlds, the implications are not only meant to indicate class, caste (as in India), or social ranking, but also a standard to aspire to by all who value and wish to propagate civility, peace, and harmony.

The Buddha makes reference to speech, which is **appropriate** and **inappropriate**. Classically, the texts are written in a way that addresses inappropriate first, but here I shall present them side by side, as the appropriate is really just the opposite of the obvious inappropriate. The illustrations made have to do with religion, faith, and spiritual matters. I shall make references here more global by including more "worldly" examples.

Firstly, have you taken the first and second Wise Action steps to determine if your audience will be receptive to what it is you want to say? In the world of AA and the 12 steps of recovery, there is mention made of making amends when it would not cause harm. Just because something is either objectively or subjectively true or it is your honest assessment or view, do you think your audience either wants or would be receptive to what you have to say? In this way you skillfully approach the situation, which will, even in the most challenging instance, hopefully yield the results you want or will at least mollify whatever negative consequences may arise. For, we must always keep in mind that relative reality is slippery and unless we are fully enlightened and prescient, there will be unintended consequences and interpretations, perceived implications, and so forth.

Secondly, how clear are you in your intentions to say what you have to say? With intentions that are clearly considered beforehand, this will often help you to hone what it is you want and do not want to present and how to prioritize.

Along those lines, is what you are about to say relevant to what is needed for you to achieve what you are intending to achieve? Your digressions into other matters may be something you have not well considered. But, besides wasting another's time, they can also be viewed as deliberate subterfuge or distractions.

Finally, as a refinement of the first point on what is appropriate or inappropriate, how well have you assessed through the first three Wise Action steps as to whether what you have to say is relevant or of interest to those whom you are about to address? The third Wise Action step, "reflect," with respect to your own experience of the issue or matter to be discussed, also has an interesting neuroscience dimension with respect to mirror neurons. Simply stated, if you are in integrity within yourself on a subject or issue, you will implicitly have a sense or intuition as to whether the audience will be receptive or not. That is, the more you "read" yourself, the more you can "read" your audience.

The Anguttara Nikaya warns **not to initiate arguments**.[4] Arguments can arise for any number of reasons, but they are usually tainted by the third poison – aggression. The Buddha forewarns us that if we engage or initiate aggressive speech, one can expect five outcomes. Outcomes one and two are that not only may your efforts not amount to anything beneficial, but if you have previously gained trust, accomplished something positive, whatever you have gained will fall apart. Thirdly, you will ruin your own reputation amongst others, and as a result, your credibility and the willingness for others to engage you will diminish. The fourth outcome is that it weakens your mental and physical state. Have you ever noticed how drained you feel after you have had an angry outburst? The Buddha says, "Anger destroys virtue." Virtue is usually embodied by physical well-being and mental clarity. It is almost as if all that energy you have put into reasoning an argument results in your mind becoming weaker, and as such, you are left in a greater state of confusion. Whether you adhere to a philosophy that embraces future lives, the Buddha warns of finding yourself in the future being in what could be defined as a hellish state with the hallmark characteristic being in a heightened level of confusion.

The Buddha realized that whenever looking at any given situation, you need to apply the Five Steps of Wise Action. By scrutinizing a situation thus, there is greater likelihood that the **praise or blame** you assign another will be true and have merit. That said, in all matters, the assignment of praise and blame is always complicated for two reasons. First, relative reality always has opposing views on what is good, bad, etc. You never have the full picture and – if not fully awakened yourself – you cannot see down the road as to what outcomes may arise from what is said or what is done. Secondly, if you, yourself, are not spotless and free of projection, how well are you judging the situation? With this in mind, it is far better not to assign praise and blame than to do so. Of course, this does not mean that you should never offer a compliment or criticism. But, again, have you done an honest assessment on your own part before offering such? And furthermore, the Buddha says that whether you offer a compliment or a criticism, along with whether these are accurate and true, **timing** should also be considered. One needs to be wary of **any** rush to judgment, positive or negative. A poorly-timed compliment may inhibit the completion of an action, lead to laziness, or an inflated sense of self. A disparaging remark said prematurely may inhibit an action, which, if followed through, may lead to a positive outcome.

Covert, secret, or privileged communications demand a higher level of propriety and timing. Is what is said in this way idle or spurious gossip that leads to confusion, even harm? If not, if it is true, does it need to be held in trust and only shared in such circles with which this information is useful and can lead to greater benefit if held in such a way? Is there greater virtue in this information being shared? Is there an appropriate, larger audience? Is it time sensitive?

In the Majjhima Nikaya, the Buddha raises these questions not only for covert speech, but also what Bhikkhu Bodhi translates as "overt sharp speech." To both, the Buddha says, "… when one knows overt sharp speech [or covert speech] to be true, correct, and beneficial, one may utter it, knowing the time to do so."[5]

Thus, with the Five Steps of Wise Action applied, even the most seemingly uncivil speech can be civil.

What may be considered the most challenging form of speech to render civil is what Bhikkhu Bodhi touches upon last in his section devoted to proper speech. The issue is **the reproaching of another**. In the Anguttara Nikaya, rather than the Buddha himself speaking, the words uttered come from one of his disciples, the Venerable Sariputra. Although Sariputra is addressing monks, the same five points regarding the admonishing of another apply as the most civil way to do so in any circumstance.

(1) He should consider: "I will speak at a proper time, not at an improper time; (2) I will speak truthfully, not falsely; (3) I will speak gently, not harshly; (4) I will speak in a beneficial way, not in a harmful way; (5) I will speak with a mind of loving kindness, not while harboring hatred."[6]

But what if one is at the receiving end of being reproached? Here, the Buddha says that regardless of how that reproach is delivered, listen to it with no malice and assess the truth of what is being said on the merit of the facts. If you find what is said to be true, take heed and work to overcome what is unskillful in your own speech and action. If you act accordingly, more than likely the fact that you heeded the reproach will, in the future, make the one who did so unto you, an ally.

When you study the material from chapter on President Washington's "Rules of Civility," you will easily observe the universality of this wisdom and skill in speech and action as shared here. As the adage goes, "There is nothing new under the sun." We are merely called to make relevant and useful in our lives what has always been true.

Chapter Four

Mind Training and Civility

At the end of the tenth century and into the eleventh century CE, there was a Buddhist teacher from India by the name of Atisha (982-1054 CE). During the most significant and lasting revitalization of Buddhism in Tibet, in what is known as the Tibetan Renaissance from 950-1200 CE, the teachings of Atisha were highly regarded and influential. Atisha codified and introduced the Buddha's teachings on mind training, which became known as *lojong* (which simply means "mind training") in a series of easy-to-remember slogans. In this training, there were both contemplations and meditative exercises, designed to engender deep wisdom and compassion. These teachings have been adopted and adapted by all the schools of Tibetan Buddhism.

Atisha's original 59 slogans of Mind Training were subdivided into seven main categories or points. The full text of these slogans can be found in the Appendix at the end of this book. Note that many if not most of the slogans are universally useful for anyone wanting to develop wisdom and compassion, as was Atisha's intent. To this, I would add that the end result would be a very civil person. Thus, here I wish to only focus on those slogans which seem most appropriate to look at within the context of civility and civil action. I am indebted to the Nalanda Translation Committee, established by the late Ven. Chögyam Trungpa Rinpoche, for their translation of these slogans. Note that the wording of each slogan is italicized and indicates that the Committee's translation is what is being used, hence unaltered.

Each slogan as translated by the translation committee will be in quotes and italicized. Note that at the end of each slogan cited, I shall offer commentary that will be identified as such.

The First Point of mind training focuses on a four-fold meditation which goes by various names: "The Four Thoughts that turn the mind to the Dharma" (or the teachings of the Buddha), "The Four Thoughts that turn the mind to spirituality." The one I like is "The Four Thoughts that Revolutionize the Mind."

These four thoughts are classified together as the first slogan and are…

1. *"Maintain an awareness of the preciousness of human life."*
    COMMENTARY: How much do you appreciate your own life? If you cannot engage the world with this appreciation, then civility is hard to embody, and if feigned, will be shallow at best.
2. *"Be aware of the reality that life ends; death comes for everyone; Impermanence."*
    COMMENTARY: Without a notion of impermanence, it is impossible to relax or let go. Thus, desperation and insistence become more fanatical. And, life becomes humorless. Civility is then tainted with desperation or resignation.
3. *"Recall that whatever you do, whether virtuous or not, has a result; Karma."*
    COMMENTARY: In keeping with the Biblical, "What you sow, so shall you reap"; that how you engage a person or a situation will eventually come back to you in some reciprocal way. Therefore, the adage of civility in this light is "Treat others as you would like to be treated." And, if you don't then remember, "what goes around comes around."
4. *"Contemplate that as long as you are too focused on self-importance and too caught up in thinking about how you are good or bad, you will experience suffering. Obsessing about*

*getting what you want and avoiding what you don't want does
not result in happiness; Ego."*
COMMENTARY: Without an altruistic spirit, civility is
not possible. Self-importance or only looking out for your
own advantage or success will bankrupt the situation.

Point Two focuses on an awakened consciousness. Known in
Sanskrit as *bodhicitta*, we more precisely reside with a heart that
is awakened to the call of compassion. There is what is called
absolute bodhicitta and relative bodhicitta. Absolute bodhicitta is
about the actual state of our mind and our deep spiritual desires
or intentions. Relative bodhicitta is about how we express this
through our **Five Steps to Wise Action** and the **Four Levels of
Compassion**.

Regarding *Absolute Bodhicitta*
Slogan 4. *"Self-liberate even the antidote."*
COMMENTARY: Be wary of becoming rigid or dogmatic.
Just because something works one time does not mean it
will work **all** the time. Maintain your flexibility.
Slogan 5. *"Rest in the nature of alaya, the essence, the present
moment."*
COMMENTARY: If you can stay present to what is in
front of you, you become less under the sway of the Three
Poisons. Your civility should have a sense of openness
and possibility.

Regarding *Relative Bodhicitta*
Slogan 7. *"Sending and taking should be practiced alternately.
These two should ride the breath (aka practice Tonglen)."*
COMMENTARY: This is an excellent meditation practice
to train in and will be discussed in the conclusion of this
chapter.
Slogan 8. *"Three objects, three poisons, three roots of virtue –*

The 3 objects are friends, enemies and neutrals. The 3 poisons are craving, aversion and indifference. The 3 roots of virtue are the remedies."

COMMENTARY: A reminder that civil action and speech is thwarted most by the Three Poisons: ignorance, attachment, and aggression. Here, *craving* is associated with attachment, *aversion* to aggression, and *indifference* to ignorance. Here we see the more active way in which ignorance can also be expressed in our willful ignoring or disregard. Such inattentiveness is a barrier to true engagement in civil discourse.

Slogan 9. *"In all activities, train with slogans."*

COMMENTARY: Having slogans or easy-to-remember phrases to remind oneself of the type of behavior one wishes to exhibit is quite helpful, especially in the beginning of cultivating your civility in all circumstances.

Slogan 10. *"Begin the sequence of sending and taking with yourself."*

COMMENTARY: This is in keeping with **reflection**, as connected to mirror-like wisdom in the Five Steps to Wise Action. Furthermore, by starting with yourself and showing yourself some *mercy*, there is greater likelihood that such kindness will influence your interactions.

Point Three, the "Transformation of Bad Circumstances into the Way of Enlightenment," is far reaching. Everyone could benefit from the views and the practices that allow one to see the world in this way. But, I wish to focus on a few, more basic points as others go deep into Buddhist meditative practices and philosophy.

Slogan 11. *"When the world is filled with evil, transform all mishaps into the path of bodhi."*

COMMENTARY: In colloquial terms, if presented with

lemons, do your best to make lemonade. Every situation is workable. Can you apply the Five Steps of Wise Action to figure out how to best approach what would otherwise be seen as an unworkable situation from the Three Poison viewpoint?

Slogan 12. *"Drive all blames into one."*

COMMENTARY: Whenever a situation or interaction is not working out, if possible make the first step the third of the Five Steps of Wisdom: **reflect**. What is your part? Furthermore, if you start from there, you may actually find out that the situation becomes more workable much more quickly than going out on the attack.

Slogan 13. *"Be grateful to everyone."*

COMMENTARY: We are all children of God living on the same planet, trying to do our best. If we start with such a perspective and celebrate the opportunity we face, then civility naturally becomes part of the transaction.

Slogan 16. *"Whatever you meet unexpectedly, join with meditation."*

COMMENTARY: The greater the challenge, the more important openness and flexibility will be in order to maintain a civil approach. Meditative awareness is an important tool here.

The Fifth Point asks one to be reflective on how one is doing with Mind Training. All four of the slogans of this Point are cogent.

Slogan 19. *All dharma agrees at one point.*

COMMENTARY: This has to do with overcoming our habitual preoccupation with our own views and desires. In civility, for our transactions to be "on the level," it is imperative that we are able to work with others where their needs and opinions are respected and dealt with in a way that is illustrative of that perspective.

Slogan 20. *Of the two witnesses, hold the principal one.*
To this, the Nalanda Committee explains: "You know yourself better than anyone else knows you."
COMMENTARY: To be civil, you have to be honest about your own experience. The Ven. Chögyam Trungpa taught, "First thought, best thought," a point I share in *The Passionate Buddha*. What this means is that you may not know all the facts, but if you are not honest about how you see them and second-guess yourself, more than likely this diversion will actually lead you further from both the truth and your ability to maintain a civil dialogue.

Slogan 21. *Always maintain only a joyful mind.*
COMMENTARY: As explained in an earlier chapter, Tibetans use the same word for *joy* and *discipline*. That is, you really need to train your mind and develop a wider view. It does not come just on its own, unless you have transformed the habits that would otherwise lead you down a darker path. That said, our Path of Civility is one in which discipline must be applied.

Slogan 22. *If you can practice even when distracted, you are well trained.*
COMMENTARY: Can you keep your cool, no matter how hot the passions are to respond otherwise?

In Points Six and Seven, we look at the daily behaviors that support a more awakened approach to living and acting in the world followed by those behaviors and attitudes we need to employ when trying to master our minds in order to fully embody our basic goodness, the root of civility. Commentary will be necessary for some of the following slogans. But there are some that will just be obvious and need no further embellishment. In these slogans you will see similarities with many of "The Rules of Civility" which George Washington endeavored to live by and encourage in others.

> Slogan 23. *Always abide by the three basic principles –*
> *Dedication to your practice, refraining from outrageous*
> *conduct, developing patience.*
> COMMENTARY: In the basic slogan and the added
> commentary, the reminder is that time, persistence and
> patience can accomplish much. Civility is not only in the
> moment, but also in the pacing that it often takes for new
> ideas and actions to sink in, make sense, and be acted
> upon or responded to.
> Slogan 24. *Change your attitude, but remain natural.*
> COMMENTARY: Acting civil should never be in quotes
> (i.e. "civil"). The greater the contrivance, the greater the
> annoyance in response.
> Slogan 25. *Don't talk about injured limbs.*
> COMMENTARY: More often than not, people know what
> is wrong with them or in a given situation. Harping on
> these points usually just adds insult to the injury.
> Slogan 26. *Don't ponder others.*
> COMMENTARY: The third of the Five Steps of Wise
> Action is to **reflect**. How well do you know yourself?
> If you are aware how hard it is for you to know or be
> honest with yourself, how accurate and how useful is
> it to second-guess others? That said, if you do develop
> the skills to know yourself well and come from integrity
> as you go to the next Action Step, to **engage**, more than
> likely your knowledge of them will be far better informed
> and useful.
> Slogan 27. *Work with the greatest defilements first.*
> COMMENTARY: In civil discourse or action, have you
> taken the Action steps to **step back** and **assess**? What are
> the greatest *defilements* or barriers to civility here?
> Slogan 28. *Abandon any hope of fruition.*

COMMENTARY: You may have a desired outcome for a transaction. But, if it is too rigidly defined, you will miss the possibilities in the moment. In terms of your civility skills, too much attention on this will lead you away from the moment and authentic quality contact.

Slogan 29. *Abandon poisonous food.*

COMMENTARY: Associate yourself with those who support healthy, positive outcomes. And, be aware of your own internal habitual dialogues that may lead you to act from a negative emotional state such as anger, jealousy, etc...

Slogan 30. *Don't be so predictable.*

COMMENTARY: Relative or conditional reality is never cut and dry. You need openness and flexibility in thinking and acting.

Slogan 31. *Don't malign others.*

COMMENTARY: Maligning others will lead to malignancy.

Slogan 32. *Don't wait in ambush.*

COMMENTARY: Strategizing to take advantage of another and their vulnerabilities is cowardly as well as uncivil.

Slogan 33. *Don't bring things to a painful point.*

COMMENTARY: Only if we are in a situation where we need to apply the Fourth Level of Compassion, wrathfulness, does this situation warrant consideration. To start out or direct things to an unpleasant point beforehand is unskillful and demonstrates the lack of compassion so vital to civil engagement.

Slogan 34. *Don't transfer the ox's load to the cow.*

COMMENTARY: In our first two Wise Action steps, we should be able to discern who is responsible for what. Keep this clear. Know and accept what you are culpable for.

Slogan 35. *Don't try to be the fastest.*

COMMENTARY: The Path of Civility is to expand possibility by developing consensus rooted in all being on the level. We are deliberately focused on a win-win scenario. We are not trying to better someone, but rather, make it better for all whenever possible.

Slogan 36. *Don't act with a twist.*

COMMENTARY: If a discourse or action is going in the direction you want or intend, don't try to seize the initiative and make it more or more to the disadvantage of the other.

Slogan 37. *Don't turn gods into demons.*

COMMENTARY: You should not drag someone down so that you can look somehow better, superior, and more right... Let their actions and words stand on their own. In the end, our own Three Poisons are the source of our downfall.

Slogan 38. *Don't seek others' pain as the limbs of your own happiness.*

COMMENTARY: Remember the old Welsh saying: "If you plan revenge, dig two graves."

Slogan 39. *All activities should be done with one intention.*

COMMENTARY: Coming out of our altruistic heart, we try to keep the focus for our transactions being "For the goodness of all concerned."

Slogan 40. *Correct all wrongs with one intention.*

COMMENTARY: Refer to Slogan 39.

Slogan 45. *Take on the three principal causes: the teacher, the dharma, the sangha.*

COMMENTARY: It is good to seek out mentors and/or examples of the kind of person you want to be when conversing and acting in the world. Similarly, take time to study and find others who wish to share a similar civil culture to you.

Slogan 46. *Pay heed that the three never wane.*
COMMENTARY: Keep a positive, grateful attitude. These will reinforce your efforts.

Slogan 49. *Always meditate on whatever provokes resentment.*
COMMENTARY: Those issues, attitudes or words of others that provoke the most reactivity in you, stimulating your Three Poisons, are your best teachers. They show you the edges of what you have and have not yet accomplished on The Path. Whatever the strong emotion, do your best to face and transform it. Bring it to the Path where you use your Five Steps of Wise Action to determine the best Level of Compassion to deploy.

Slogan 50. *Don't be swayed by external circumstances.*
COMMENTARY: Training in equanimity in all circumstances ensures that the civility you practice will be the most appropriate and effective.

Slogan 51. *This time, practice the main points: others before self, dharma, and awakening compassion.*
COMMENTARY: Train to remain in touch with and steadfast in your basic goodness.

Slogan 52. *Don't misinterpret.* The Nalanda Committee summarizes so succinctly, their comment leaves no need for further commentary. "The six things that may be misinterpreted are patience, yearning, excitement, compassion, priorities and joy. You're patient when you're getting your way, but not when it's difficult. You yearn for worldly things, instead of an open heart and mind. You get excited about wealth and entertainment, instead of your potential for enlightenment. You have compassion for those you like, but none for those you don't. Worldly gain is your priority rather than cultivating loving-kindness and compassion. You feel joy when your enemies suffer, and do not rejoice in others' good fortune."

Slogan 53. *Don't vacillate* (in your practice of Mind Training).

Slogan 54. *Train wholeheartedly.*

Slogan 55. *Liberate yourself by examining and analyzing: Know your own mind with honesty and fearlessness.*

Slogan 56. *Don't wallow in self-pity.*

COMMENTARY: Self-pity for what positive qualities you may lack or self-denigration, berating yourself for not being perfect right now, will sabotage your efforts at mindful self-improvement. Be civil with **yourself**.

Slogan 57. *Don't be jealous.*

COMMENTARY: Jealousy undermines self-confidence and self-worth. Communicating from such a mind-set will make others wary of communicating with you in the first place. Neither will it engender confidence in those with whom you interact.

Slogan 58. *Don't be frivolous.*

COMMENTARY: Measure the tone and tenor of what is best for the situation. Stay honest. Stay in integrity.

Slogan 59. *Don't expect applause.*

COMMENTARY: The Path of Civility yields its own rewards.

Tong Len Meditation: The Practice of Taking and Sending

Atisha's Slogans 53 and 54 encourage a general appreciation and perseverance in Mind Training, but especially this meditation technique. It is founded upon the observation, contemplation, and meditation, whereby we realize that nothing lives in isolation. We are inseparable from everyone and everything around us and this at-oneness. Furthermore, in our interconnectedness, we see that we are always as much a part of the problem as we are part of the solution. So, even if we cannot solicit the participation of others in the resolving of tensions, conflicts, and problems, we can begin by working on ourselves and our relationship with others and to these difficulties. *Tong Len*, or "Taking and Sending," meditation is an excellent daily practice to help us to fully develop our relationship with what is around us and support a more civil outlook in general as we appreciate our part and how to deploy our basic goodness in all of our actions and transactions.

The Path of Civility must first and foremost begin with us becoming civil to ourselves – our foibles, our follies, and projections. According to Atisha, the first person we need to do Taking and Sending for is ourselves. There are many levels of meaning in what he is saying. At the simplest level, we realize that all of our suffering arises from our own unmitigated Three Poisons; it is therefore useful for us to breathe in and *take back* from the world around us the thoughts, words, and actions that we have committed based on ignorance, attachment, and aggression. Breathing in with this thought in mind, we place in action an intention and commitment no longer to pollute our world and those we come into contact with. As we breathe out, we send a breath of freshness, vibrancy, and good intentions out into the world.

As we come to own our projections and create more space for others, we become sensitive to their projections, the effects of the Three Poisons on them. We become more sensitive to why they are the way they are. As we breathe in, we then feel more compassion to take in and transform *their pain* and confusion, and send waves of understanding and love out to *them*. If, in the context of a seemingly intractable situation, we breathe in whatever pain, confusion, or horror we see before us along with our own projections about the situation, we create a space within us that allows us to come to a problem afresh, less burdened by the weight of history.

The Meditation

1. If you are doing this as a formal meditation, begin by sitting and adjusting your posture and breathing and come to the point where all you are doing is observing the passage of air at the tip of your nose.

2. Begin the Taking and Sending process with yourself. As you breathe in, put your intention and commitment into absorbing all of your tendencies to project ignorance, attachment, and aggression out into the world. If you are stuck at this time with any particular negative emotion, breathe it in, knowing that this emotion colors and distorts your actions. The negativity that you breathe in goes to your heart, in which there rests a deep blue ball of light. If you want, you can imagine that that ball of light hums with a particular sound: "HOONG." This light and sound are considered in Tantric tradition to be the nature of your mind. It is also very healing. You allow the Three Poisons and their projections to be dissolved and healed in the deep blue light and sound of HOONG. As you breathe out, imagine that pure, radiant love pours from your heart center, floods your entire being, then expands into and fills the space around you. Feel this radiant love as clear and WHITE, extending out as far as you can imagine.

3. Having done several breath cycles like this with yourself in mind, it is now time to bring your attention to others. Imagine that behind you are people in general, people you have no particular thought or emotion about one way or the other. Think of these people first, as you have few strong emotions or biases about them. For them, you start by focusing on their general pain and confusion. As you breathe in and out, repeat for them what you did for yourself. In your mind's eye, see their negativity come out of their bodies and minds and enter into that BLUE

light in your heart where such negativity, the Three Poisons and their residues, are dissolved and healed. Imagine this negativity as being like black tar or smoke. As you breathe out, see the radiant clear WHITE light spread into their bodies and minds, filling them with clarity, joy, and love. You are forging a closer connection to them – to humanity and all beings in general – as a result.

4. Now, focus on those with whom you have a close or personal relationship. See these people on either side of you. Imagine women you know on your left and the men on your right to make the meditation more energetically effective. Breathe in and out on their behalf in the same manner. Do this for several cycles of breath as well. You may even focus on a particular individual about whom you are concerned.

5. Now go to the next step of focusing your attention on people you have difficulty with. These can be those with whom you have a personal relationship, someone with whom you need to have a serious conversation that requires a change of heart, even a world leader. Imagine that they are sitting directly in front of you. Repeat the process for them as you did for all of the others in steps 3 and 4.

Take your time building up your strength and resolve to do this practice. Start with yourself. Gradually include others in a way that does not push you past a general sense of equanimity. There is not much value in finding yourself obsessing in the meditation about someone you love or someone you totally despise. Certainly, you want to work past these emotions to get to a place where you see a more workable relationship or situation. But it is more useful to acknowledge first where you are within yourself and build *Tong Len* slowly as an effective tool.

Besides being a formal meditation practice, *Tong Len* can be done on the spot in situations with others where there is pain or difficulty. In such circumstances, you can always breathe in and breathe out in accordance with this practice without others needing to know what you are doing. As you hold the intention of wanting to absorb rather than react to the pain, suffering, bad feelings, or confusion of the moment, this will have an effect on how you relate to the situation. In hostile situations, *Tong Len* can even dispel the tension or bring it to a resolution more quickly. In any event, you have stopped yourself, through your intention and breathing, from contributing to the problem. This can go a long way in moving relationships and situations forward. On The Path of Civility where you will be inevitably called to employ all Four Levels of Compassion, *Tong Len* will prove itself a useful personal, transformational tool.

Chapter Five

The Rules of Civility

President Washington's "Rules of Civility" were what the young Washington copied from a book, entitled, *Youth's Behaviour, Or, Decencie in Conversation Amongst Men*, by Francis Hawkins, published in 1668. The original material for Hawkins' book came from a 1595 French Jesuit text, entitled, *Bienseance de la Conversation Entre les Hommes*. Apropos for clergy and laymen, no doubt, as those who were literate at this time were of an upper class within society, this work was intended for young men of privilege. Thus, in civil society, it would have been presented to them by their parents, mentors, or teachers with the sole intent of helping their young men become pleasing, to advance, and be respected and influential. The chapter that grabbed young George's attention was "The Rules of Civility and Decent Behaviour in Company and Conversation." The manuscript of rules that he copied down was simply entitled, "Rules of Civility," with his original being preserved at the Library of Congress.

It is clear when looking at the 110 points written down by Washington that, like the title implies in the chapter in Hawkins' book, we are looking at both civility and decency, in particular decorum and propriety. Presenting oneself to others in such a refined or dignified and respectful manner goes a long way in allowing others to more willingly engage in communication with he or she who presents themselves thus. That is, one could say that decorum and propriety enhance or reinforce civility. One should note, however, that unlike civility, which is more to do specifically with communication and action, decorum and propriety are more time and culture bound; that is, they change more readily as societies and cultures evolve or – for that matter

– devolve. Thus, whereas as civility as we have defined it in the beginning of this volume is universal, decorum and propriety are more conditioned. Thus, as I elucidate the 110 points, it will be noted when a point is more of Washington's era. At the same time, there may be modern manifestations that make seemingly arcane considerations relevant here and now.

Of course, one can assume that such rules, whether they are universal or conditional, are mere conventions. However, even in the Pali Canon of the Buddha, as well as the examples we have presented with respect to speech, there are timeless lessons on personal training and cordiality and their practical usefulness in establishing social and communal harmony. That we are by nature social creatures, hence need rules of conduct and moral guidance, the Buddha, the Jesuits, Hawkins, and Washington are all in agreement.

Based on this understanding, my intention in this section is to first present the "Rules of Civility" as copied down by Washington (punctuation, grammar, spellings, and capitalizations included) and apply the wisdom and principles I have laid out according to the teachings of Buddha Sakyamuni in the form of commentary. The goal is to demonstrate how each one remains as applicable and useful for today as Washington found for his own life, in service to his country, and the greater good for which civility is a key component.

When reading the Rules, you will also note that Hawkins suggests how to be courteous, how to display civility and decorum in one's own behavior, but then also makes recommendations of the same when others are clearly not being so in relation to you. In this, I am reminded of the slogans of Atisha where he says, "Drive all blames into one." Although put in the context of poor behavior and how to view it within yourself and others, it is possible to take this slogan and use it to view what is good and virtuous. That is, be good, be an example of good, and when witnessing others not being so, be an even better example of good.

As you go through the Rules, they will at times appear to be redundant. That is, that the same point is being made in different rules. However, you will observe that most rules often contain two to three points for consideration. When presented in this way, the point that seems redundant takes on a whole new perspective, and with it, the commentary I offer will change based on the nuances of those new combinations of points that Hawkins wishes you to observe.

Lastly, the commentaries, themselves, can be viewed as contemplations. Read the Rule, and then take some time to not only ponder its directness, but also consider what nuances the commentaries point out. In this respect, the Rules and their commentaries are not only intended to make a lasting impression, but also bring about a reformation of character resulting in you being an example of civility to all.

1. "Every Action done in Company ought to be with Some Sign of Respect to those that are Present."
    Commentary: To accomplish such action requires that you know yourself and know the company you are in. If you practice some form of mindfulness discipline, then, being in a higher level of integrity within yourself, not only will that present an air that is pleasing, but you will naturally be more attentive to the responses of those around you. At the same time, if the social or political dimensions of the encounter require a higher level of decorum and/or sensitivity to social or cultural nuances of those present, then it is good to have knowledge of these aspects and/or be informed accordingly.

2. "When in Company, put not your Hands to any Part of the Body not usually Discovered."
    Commentary: Within our nervous systems, the hands cover a very large region of the brain's central sulcus.

As such, we are very cognizant of where others have their hands when in interaction with us. That said, the appearance, placement, and movement of our hands in an interaction with another speaks volumes in terms of how we perceive them and how we feel in the transaction. Are we displaying shyness, too much familiarity, awkwardness, aggression, etc.? In the East, there is even a spiritual technology around the combination of the fingers and how they are placed, where they move to, and their resultant effects on others and us. Although some of this we learn inadvertently by observation and reactions through family and so on, learning this technology (*mudra*) can actually enhance communication effectiveness.

3.   "Show Nothing to your Friend that might affright him."
Commentary: Fright or shock of this nature has its place in the spectrum of communication. "Shock value" can have its place in marketing or stopping a transaction, or moving it in a new direction. But, it has no place in civility, especially among those with whom you are either friends or those you want to cultivate as such. Whereas civility is a process of smoothing a continuum of communication, shock or fright is disruptive and will, in fact, create greater uncertainty in the transactions that may follow.

4.   "In the Presence of Others, Sing not to yourself with a humming Noise, nor Drum with your Fingers or Feet."
Commentary: Distracting oneself through these behaviors demonstrates a lack of a level of personal awareness as to what one is doing, but also that one is not fully paying attention to the other/s. There can be biochemical reasons, some of which one may not be able to control, but others can be (i.e. intoxication, too much sugar, etc...). In these times, we can easily add a

preoccupation with tiny screens and other digital media that so often people continue to stay plugged into, even in the middle of a face-to-face conversation that they are engaged in. There can also be mental/emotional distractions that one cannot shake in oneself – perhaps even attitudes towards the others in your presence. A mindfulness practice, where you learn to still the body and mind, can be quite useful to stem, reduce, even curtail such outward distracting behaviors.

5. "If you Cough, Sneeze, Sigh, or Yawn, do it not Loud but Privately; and Speak not in your Yawning, but put your handkerchief or Hand before your face and turn aside."

Commentary: In the medical systems of the East of which the historical Buddha was familiar, there are treatises, which say that the suppression of such reflexive bodily urges is injurious to the health. However, in popular culture, it is almost as if "doubling down" by making these actions a feature in the discourse is somehow acceptable, if not oddly "cool." But, they bespeak a familiarity or casualness that adds little, but often lessens or diminishes the impact of what we are trying to communicate. On the flip side, if such urges do arise, the act of concealing, turning, etc. may, in fact, enhance the moment by its humanity and convey a respect for the situation.

6. "Sleep not when others Speak, Sit not when others stand, Speak not when you Should hold your Peace, Walk not on when others Stop."

Commentary: Essentially what we are talking about here is (a) how well you know the situation you find yourself in, and (b) are you paying attention? Of the two, paying attention is primary. With a relaxed and focused mind, so many indiscretions and offenses can be naturally avoided. Furthermore, if you can be apprised of the situation and protocol accordingly, all the better.

7. "Put not off your Cloths in the presence of Others, nor go out your Chamber half Dressed."

    Commentary: How one is dressed is about decorum and propriety. But, again, as expressed earlier being well dressed, groomed well, etc. dignifies the situation and encourages a higher level of attention and interaction. Of course, vanity, modesty, etc., i.e. more personal reasons may be at play in one's mind. There may also be cultural factors as to what is appropriate in public and what is not. In this latter point, what you consider to be appropriate in public or to the situation may not be what another party may consider so. And in this we get into issues of the freedom of personal expression – something we in the West consider a high priority. However, if we are practicing the 5 Steps of Wise Action – step back, assess, reflect, engage, enact – our decision to be in public in accordance with the time and circumstance we find ourselves in is less tied to our personal or egoist proclivities.

8. "At Play and at Fire, it's Good manners to Give Place to the last Comer, and affect not to Speak Louder than Ordinary."

    Commentary: Courtesy or showing deference because of age, rank, honors, disability, etc. does not contradict the notion that we are ultimately all of equal standing. Depending on time and circumstance, those who are given preference can change. Such respect in these circumstances sets a civil – if not naturally gentle – tone to proceedings. Conversely, when someone expects such treatment, that air and/or irritation if not being "honored" as such will, ultimately, undermine whatever is to come next or the memory or manner in which the next encounter is anticipated or received. In communication, to "Speak Louder" than those with whom one is with is to make your own contribution more important than the others who are present. Of course, there are exceptions, like impending danger, telling a joke, etc... which would not be considered "ordinary" speech transactions.

9. "Spit not in the Fire, nor Stoop low before it, neither Put your Hands into the Flames to warm them, nor Set your Feet upon the Fire especially if there be meat before it." Commentary: Unlike the central heating of modern homes, a fire was not only for warmth, but also for cooking, the drying of clothes in inclement weather, and the place where families would gather for various social/communal activities and interactions. Thus if one wanted to spend time in conversation, in a home or a more public setting where the fire and hearth was a gathering point, the familiarity with which family members may use a fire would, more than likely, create a familiarity which may degrade the civility of the gathering and the purpose for which it was gathered.

10. "When you Sit down, Keep your Feet firm and Even, without putting one on the other or Crossing them." Commentary: In the tradition of meditation and the psychology of body language, such recommendations are quite prudent when it comes to civility. In teaching meditation, when a person cannot sit in a cross-legged position on the ground, one is taught to sit upright in a chair in the manner described. Tibetan Buddhist teacher Venerable Chögyam Trungpa used to speak of sitting with "good head and shoulders," which applied to meditation in a chair, but also as a way of displaying a quality of uprightness and dignity in the presence of

others. With respect to crossing one leg over the other when sitting, the body language experts see this as a more casual pose, but also one that blocks the "energy" between you and another person, like putting up a fence and standing behind it. That is, it creates distance, which – in the interest of equitable conversing – is inhibiting.

11. "Shift not yourself in the Sight of others nor Gnaw your nails."

    Commentary: Quietude of body in the presence of others can be reassuring. It can also be unnerving to those unaccustomed to a demeanor, which shows mastery of body and mind. Such a demeanor allows one to be more attentive.

    There can be many reasons why such a presentation of self is more challenging. The reasons can be biochemical, like too much caffeine or sugar, worms (in Oriental medicine it is said that chewing on one's nails can be a behavioral sign of having worms in the gut). There can also be mental/emotional issues – agitation, anxiety, and so on. In both regards, learning better dietary habits and learning how to meditate quietly can be quite instructive.

12. "Shake not the head, or Legs, Roll not the Eyes, Lift not one eyebrow higher than the other, Wry not the mouth, and Bedew no man's face with your Spittle, by approaching too near when you Speak."

    Commentary: With the exception to spitting on someone (unless it is intended!), all the other mannerisms described usually show or communicate a judgment on what is being conveyed in a transaction and these judgments are usually negative or come with a conflicting emotion. Yet, these responses are usually habitual and/or reflexive. One does not go out of one's way to display such. Thus, one could say that young George was taking a lesson from British aristocracy in being trained and/or disciplined to keep a "stiff upper lip" and all of the repressive mannerisms of British high society. Displaying a "poker face" or one that does not display any of the mannerisms above is useful in many social and political environs. However, in the extreme and as an expected norm, they can also be detrimental to sound mental health, both for the person inhibiting and those before them who remain more in the dark as to what one may be thinking.

In modern times, with the increased use of Botox to eliminate wrinkles, it has been noted that many reflexive facial responses are being overly inhibited via this toxin. The result is that people looking at the Botoxed face are flummoxed by what they can and cannot see. And, as a result the person with the Botoxed face cannot read the other person's response either. Thus, the ability to judge what is going on in the mind and emotions of another is said to be impaired by about fifty percent; an actual decrease in emotional intelligence.

As regards unintended spittle, especially in most civil discourse, respecting another individual's personal space will usually ensure that such "bedewing" is less likely.

13. "Kill no Vermin as fleas, lice, ticks, etc. in the Sight of Others. If you See any filth or thick Spittle put your foot Dexterously upon it. If it be upon the Cloths of your Companions, Put it off privately, and if it be upon your own Cloths, return Thanks to him who puts it off."

Commentary: There are appearances on oneself or companions or in the immediate environment that you are in which can be uplifting or degrading. And thus while it is true that beauty is relative and purity or beauty of thought, speech, and conduct is far more important, to keep beauty in mind in all ways can accentuate their affects. To have it in mind not to offend, to go out of your way to tend to another or to the circumstance so that they do not offend, and if another attends to you similarly – if done in a spirit of cordiality – can be quite sublime.

14. "Turn not your Back to others especially in Speaking, Jog not the Table or Desk on which Another reads or writes, lean not upon any one."

Commentary: If one truly wants to engage in a mutual and courteous interaction, be mindful of body language that demonstrates directness rather than secrecy or disregard – be it intentional or casual – attentiveness to the activity of the other, and neither showing a posture of dominance, submission, or too much familiarity.

15. "Keep your Nails clean and Short, also your Hands and Teeth Clean, yet without Showing any great Concern for them."

Commentary: Hygiene should be considered natural and ongoing, thus nothing that indicates that a fuss was made to present oneself in a clean and respectful way.

16. "Do not Puff up the Cheeks, Loll not out the tongue, rub the Hands, or beard, thrust out the lips, or bite them, or keep the Lips too open or too Close."

Commentary: So many of these gestures and responses are reflexive or so subconsciously habitual that it takes more of a conscious rather than obsessively rigid mind to not display such. How much do we note our body responses to nervousness, distraction, worry, confusion and so on? At the same time, with mindfulness training coupled with behavioral modification, even acting or performance training, many mannerisms like these and others referenced in other rules can be lessened, even eliminated. But, the fact that they are mostly subconscious does demand that without a more contemplative/mindfulness approach, such mannerisms and displays may take on deeper, more problematic manifestations.

17. "Be no Flatterer, neither Play with any that delights not to be Play'd Withal."

Commentary: It may be thought that everyone likes to be flattered. But, unnecessary or excessive flattery or flattery offered to a person who has discomfort in such usually breeds suspicion of the flatterer. Similarly, to engage someone playfully or encourage someone to play who clearly is not in the mood generally evokes irritation. It may even be taken as an insult or gesture bespeaking an attitude of some sort of superiority.

18. "Read no Letters, Books, or Papers in Company but when there is a Necessity for doing of it you must ask leave: come near the Books or Writings of Another so as to read them unless desired, or give your opinion of them unasked; also look not nigh when another is writing a letter."

Commentary: Having someone stay on their handheld device while speaking or listening to one or staying hooked to a blue-tooth speaker and microphone are almost universal in the digitally addicted second and first worlds. We almost never know how much someone is hearing fully what we are saying. It may even be that while connected to a blue-tooth speaker, a companion makes a comment that almost seems absurd, out of context, even beside the point – when in fact they are not responding to you, but to another. Misunderstandings, feeling unheard, and various reactive emotions like frustration and anger become more commonplace. Even more absurd is when you react to what someone says while they are engaged with another somewhere else and them feeling like you are eavesdropping. In desperation not to feel like we are missing out on something/everything, we sadly lose out on connecting fully with anything. Within two generations of digital communication as a dominant feature in daily life, we have now created classes for those who need to learn to speak one on one, eye to eye.

19. "Let your Countenance be pleasant, but in Serious Matters somewhat grave."

Commentary: To cultivate a pleasant countenance is to cultivate what I have described as Equanimitous Wisdom, where one is neither overtly reactive to highs and lows of mood, experiences, circumstances, etc. Such a perspective grows with maturity and understanding. With respect to the grave demeanor, we are talking about being in consonance with the mood of the time. To not be so, like being giddy in a sad situation, often perplexes others and generates awkwardness and uncertainty. As mentioned earlier in the commentary on Rule 12, with the growth of plastic surgery and the use of Botox, there is even more of a challenge as the nuances of facial muscles in response to emotion messages become distorted artificially. Thus, in circumstances where there is a priority to know how someone genuinely feels, if it is observed that they have indeed had such alterations, it becomes a necessity to ask for clarification.

20. "The Gestures of the Body must be Suited to the discourse you are upon."

Commentary: This succinctly reiterates my commentary on the previous point.

21. "Reproach none for the Infirmities of Nature, nor Delight to Put them that have in mind Thereof."

Commentary: Sadly, mockery of this sort has entered

into the social and political spheres, perpetuating stereotypes and causing general harm. To stand by and join in vicariously or remaining silent when such is being done not only makes oneself culpable, but diminishes one's character and sense of self-esteem.

22. "Show not yourself glad at the Misfortune of another, though he were your enemy."

Commentary: If we truly believe that we are all basically good and that we are all doing the best based on what we know, we must understand that as misguided as we may think others are in what they say and do, they think the same as us. This is the predicament of conditioned existence. And in whatever conflict we face, whether it is a personal conflict or an all-out conflagration consuming a continent, to rejoice in the pain and suffering of others shows a shallow understanding of humanity and life in general.

In the tradition of honorable warfare, the Ven. Chögyam Trungpa said that on the battlefield, after striking down a foe, a noble soldier would sit with his defeated adversary and pray with him, as he would drift into death.

Thus civility holds no quarter for those who seek revenge or take pleasure in the demise of others. Such an attitude can only diminish us as individuals and in the end, leave us prey to the same. As the previously-noted Welsh saying goes: "If you plan revenge, dig two graves."

23. "When you see a Crime punished, you may be inwardly pleased, but always show Pity to the Suffering Offender."

Commentary: Following on from Rule 22, by "inwardly pleased," it would seem in the spirit of what is said that this does not mean to be happy. When justice is served, when a punishment fits the crime, we acknowledge that that which was done will hopefully serve two criteria. First, that such was done for a greater good, and second, that the punishment is instructive, informative, and meted out with a recognition of our shared human birthright. And if it be that the punishment is punitive in nature even to the point of death, that such acts are performed with a forgiving heart and sense of remorse for the need to act thus.

24. "Do not laugh too loud or too much at any Public Spectacle."

Commentary: Of course, laughter, like many emotional responses, is quite reflexive. One can certainly modulate it to fit the circumstance. But beyond this modulation, the essential point of this rule is to not make a "Spectacle" of oneself. In the midst of mirth, unless there is a point or intention served by making oneself noticed, it is more "civil" and situation appropriate to allow oneself to be just a part of the merriment rather than a prominent feature of it.

25. "Superfluous Complements and all Affectation of Ceremony are to be avoided, yet where due they are not to be Neglected."

Commentary: Pomp for pomp's sake as well as compliments that are either unwarranted or intended to inflate another's ego for one's own designs do nothing to elevate the situation. Pretentiousness creates an environment of inauthenticity. Like poison upstream, it will undermine what follows.

Conversely, where ceremony is warranted or elevates the circumstance and where true compliments bring about recognition of something or someone to be celebrated, warmth and cordiality are usually the results.

26. "In Pulling off your Hat to Persons of Distinction, as

Noblemen, Justices, Churchmen, etc. make a Reverence, bowing more or less according to the Custom of the Better Bred, and Quality of the Person. Amongst your equals, expect not always that they Should begin with you first, but to Pull off the Hat when there is no need is Affectation, in the Manner of Saluting and re-saluting in words keep to the most usual custom."

Commentary: In a modern world where propriety, decorum, and deference fly in the face of politically correct egalitarianism and casual living, gestures of respect to those deemed worthy of deference seem pointless at best, offensive and degrading at worst. But, when we see noble actions or experience excellent qualities in another, we do feel compelled to make some gesture of acknowledgement. Thus, such gestures do have a natural human component with respect to affection and so forth that then become embellished with the time and the perspectives of the culture. Furthermore, like Rule 25, there is an admonition not to gesture thus described for no purpose or as an affectation, which would render the gesture meaningless or a mockery of sorts.

27.   "'Tis ill manners to bid one more eminent than yourself be covered, as well as to do it to whom it's due. Likewise, he that makes too much haste to Put on his hat does not well, yet he ought to Put it on at the first, or at most the Second time of being asked; now what is herein Spoken, of Qualification in behavior in Saluting, ought also to be observed in taking of Place, and Sitting down for ceremonies without Bounds is troublesome."

Commentary: In a world where cultures meet and periodically collide, it would be nice if there was just one set of rules regarding whom to stand for, whom to sit, when, where, and how. But, the simple fact is that each culture has its pecking orders and priorities when it comes to propriety, decorum, etc... The best advice is to note that such actions and gestures do have a universal quality that one can cultivate through a mindfulness perspective rooted in love and respect. Thus, one will best be able to apply the convention of the day in the most authentic way if such attitudes are the basis of your action. And, if the actions displayed are heartfelt, even if they are inaccurately or improperly enacted, those who truly are of a noble character will more than likely be forgiving of the transgression.

28. "If any one come to Speak to you while you are Sitting, stand up though he be your Inferior, and when you Present Seats, let it be to every one according to his Degree."

Commentary: To meet someone (in keeping with the principles of Freemasonry) "on the level," as it were, is to make whatever discourse that transpires on a footing that demonstrates a respect for the very act of conversing and whatever the opinion is of the person you are conversing with. At the same time, if they approached you while being in a lower position than them, by standing, you negate intimidation as a prominent feature, regardless of whether this was their intention or not.

Regarding the second point, when offering someone a seat, here the deference of the day is considered most appropriate. Here, you are both recognizing their rank or position while simultaneously bringing things down to the same level as such. There is, thus, recognition of that distinction that is respectful and, at the same time, equalizing. Hence, you are respectfully recognizing the propriety of the day.

29. "When you meet one of Greater Quality than yourself, Stop and retire, especially if it be at a Door or any

Straight place to give way for him to Pass."
Commentary: From the Buddhist perspective, the
Ven. Chögyam Trungpa Rinpoche used to speak of
"non-referential hierarchy." This notion implied a
superior quality, whether it was in an exquisite object,
or in a person who embodied noble and inspiring
characteristics. Such qualities were considered
universal – that any one in any culture would be able
to recognize, appreciate, and show deference to such.
But, it is clear from this 17th century perspective that
we are speaking of a world of secular and religious
royalty or notables, who those of breeding and those
considered lesser and expected to show deference were
taught to acknowledge in the way described, and what
those noted in this way more than likely expected. Like
today, those who truly deserved such deference were
rare as the universal qualities with the personages of
the day did not coincide or come together all that often.
Needless to say, to not incur the ire of those deemed
"noble," one learned to act in a way that would not
offend. Furthermore, the greater disparity between
those noble qualities and those deemed as "nobles"
or "nobility" more than likely has been the fodder for
intrigue, trysts, treason, and the like. It also is noted by
the modern reader that the pronoun associated with
those of "Greater Quality" is "he."

30. "In walking, the highest Place in most Countries seems
to be on the right hand. Therefore, place yourself on the
left of him whom you desire to Honor: but if three walk
together the middest Place is the most Honorable. The
wall is usually given to the most worthy if two walk
together."
Commentary: The lesson Washington was learning
here is more than a matter of decorum. The honoring

or respect shown here is coupled with a strategy to defend. In general, our hand that we defend ourselves with is the right. Thus if your right hand or side is to the one-being-respected's left (i.e. that you are on their left side), then your right arm is closest to them which makes it easier to used be as a shield or defender. If the one honored is in the middle, then it is like they are holding court in an honored way. But, they are also more defendable. That there is a reference to them being nearer to the wall implicitly verifies that protection is being factored into the honoring and respect.

31. "If any one far Surpasses others, either in age, Estate, or Merit, yet would Place to a meaner than himself in his own lodging or elsewhere the one ought not to accept it, So he on the other part should not use much earnestness nor offer it above once or twice."

Commentary: A truly noble person may offer others the better of food, place to rest, or place or station that would otherwise be their own. Whether this gesture is genuine or a mere formality, one should graciously refuse in a manner that is respectful, but ensures that the offer is not made more than twice.

While this is respectful in a conventional cultural context, Buddhist teachings say that it may be more injurious to the person offering if their generosity is not accepted. To balance these two views, one should duly assess the situation and either accept or refuse while conveying an appreciation for the magnitude of the gesture. For in what are known as the 6 perfections (Sanskrit: *paramitas*) generosity is a high virtue, a true sign of noble intent.

32. "To one that is your equal, or not much inferior you are to give the chief Place in your Lodging and he to who 'tis offered ought at first to refuse it but at the Second

to accept though not without acknowledging his own unworthiness."

Commentary: Referring to the virtue of generosity as mentioned in Rule 31, practicing such in an appropriate way is well worth training oneself in. It shows respect, humility, and an effort to treat all as you would like to be treated. The "unworthiness" which should be conveyed by them should not be an act of feigned humility, but a respectful acknowledgement of your willingness to demonstrate and practice generosity.

33. "They that are in Dignity or in office have in all places Precedency, but whilst they are Young they ought to respect those that are their equals in Birth or other Qualities, though they have no Public charge."

Commentary: In all traditions where there is a ranking of notables, there is an understanding that it is the rank and not the person who is, in fact, being held in esteem. Those who do not remember this clearly do not understand how or why such ranking was socially and/or culturally established. In those of lesser age, this can produce entitled little brats who will more than likely rue the day they were such. If at an older age, an attitude of privilege or entitlement will certainly gain few friends of worth. Thus, to be schooled in one's non-age to be respectful to peers and elders brings honor to the title or ranking and will certainly put them in good stead for having been encouraged to take to heart such mentorship.

34. "It is good Manners to prefer them to whom we Speak before ourselves, especially if they be above us, with whom in no Sort we ought to begin."

Commentary: In a modern time of political correctness a view that caters to youth as equals in all matters, such adages as, "Speak only when you are spoken to," or "Children should be seen, but not heard," appear draconian, especially the second. Even if rank or some kind of pecking order (be it familial, aristocratic, religious…) is not in place or considered, experience and history do matter. And, there is also context. So, it might be appropriate for a child to request a breakfast cereal of their choice. But, to have the first say in when to cross a busy highway shows a lack of parenting or common sense on the part of elders who know the consequences either personally or historically. And though the child may get angry, even cry, that they did not get to say or do what they wanted then and there, the adult or parent can celebrate the fact that the child is still alive. So, while the Rule applies in more genteel settings, to enforce such without an awareness of circumstance and attention and only bow to the privilege of age or rank yields its own nest of problems that can be injurious in the immediate or stultifying in the long-term.

35. "Let your Discourse with Men of Business be Short and Comprehensive."
Commentary: Get to the point. For in truth, the longer it takes for you to get to the point, the greater the likelihood that you will be precipitating more problems or consideration that do not add but rather detract from accomplishing what one wants or what was originally desired by either or both parties.

36. "Artificers and Persons of low Degree ought not to use many ceremonies to Lords, or Others of high Degree, but Respect and highly Honor them, and those of high Degree ought to treat them with affability and Courtesy, without Arrogance."
Commentary: The issues in this Rule are matters of flattery versus due praise or legitimately due deference and civil courtesy born out of an understanding of the

privilege of place versus the arrogance of lording an air of entitlement.

37. "In speaking to men of Quality, do not lean nor in the Face, nor approach too near them; at least Keep a full Pace from them."

Commentary: "Knowing one's place" does not necessarily imply kowtowing or shrinking before another. As animals of a supposedly higher nature, we are still but animals who can feel threatened when gestures make the upper part of our body closer than the lower part of our body (like when leaning forward), when without a deeper reason in conversing we try to engage the other directly eye to eye, or with no apparent kinship that would warrant, step into another's personal space – a space we can generally sense more at a biological than cognitive level. To train to be aware of the discomfort we may engender by being too close or direct requires one to develop a mindfulness of one's own physical presence, and perception and acknowledgement of the intention that one has in being close or afar.

38. "In visiting the Sick, do not Presently play the Physician if you be not Knowing therein."

Commentary: Unless you have a role as a healer of the body, the mind, or the spirit, and the person you are visiting knows you to be or requests you to be such, it is far better to approach the sick in a way that they would expect of you. And if such services or needs arise from them, then acting in such a way will be received in accordance to what they will best be able to accept. Generally speaking unsolicited advice is rarely welcome, especially in times when kindness and just your presence would be more welcome.

39. "In writing or Speaking, give to every Person his due

Title According to his Degree and the Custom of the Place."

Commentary: Acknowledgement of others in this way, even if the content of what you are to say or write is in criticism of them, shows respect for the place or station in which society has recognized them. Thus whether words of praise or blame are uttered, there is a greater probability that your words are received in the best possible light.

40. "Strive not with your Superiors in argument, but always Submit your Judgment to others with Modesty."

Commentary: Notice that this Rule does not imply that you should shy away from argument if in argument you are with someone of rank for whom you should show deference. Rather, don't push it (i.e. "Strive") or be too strident in your case. In such circumstances, especially in the company of others who may also have the same deference to the person you are arguing with, a modest tone engenders a civil atmosphere in which disagreements may be better being investigated without the accusations of personal attack, disrespect, etc...

41. "Undertake not to Teach your equal in the art himself Professes; it Savours of arrogance."

Commentary: There is a wonderful pithy English saying: "Don't try to teach your mother how to suck eggs." The point in this saying is that you should not try to "school" someone in something they already know or are known to be skilled at. Of course, one may not know them to be skilled in such, which would make the offense just born out of ignorance, which of course one can make light of, apologize for, etc... But, if you do know, then short of being considered an arrogant "know it all," your advice or suggestions will be met with some level of irritation.

42. "Let they ceremonies in Courtesy be proper to the Dignity of his place with whom thou converses, for it is absurd to act the same with a Clown and a Prince."

Commentary: Know with who you are engaged and show them the courtesy which best demonstrates an air of respect and propriety between the two of you. Again, we go back to our original definition of civility, which then is placed in the context in which it is applied.

43. "Do not express Joy before one sick or in pain, for that contrary Passion will aggravate his Misery."

Commentary: To show empathy for the sick does not imply that one needs to be morose or glum. One can be cheerful and make efforts to be uplifting to their mood as happiness; even laughter can be a most welcome balm. But to be preoccupied or identified with one's own happiness of circumstance, etc. is not meeting the person in their hour of need in a manner that does show empathy. It may be that they would like to hear of your good news and may even want to celebrate with you as best they can. But tend to their need first as pain and hardship when met is best engaged first before all other matters are expressed or explored.

44. "When a man does all he can, though it Succeeds not well, blame not him that did it."

Commentary: This Rule acknowledges the altruistic spirit of humans and that everyone is doing their best based on what they know. Especially when an act has been done with the best possible intention, though the effort fails, a lesson is learned. If this lesson is met with blame and derision, more than likely whatever jewel there is in the lesson of failure will be lost.

45. "Being to advise or reprehend any one, consider whether it ought to be in public or in Private; presently, or at Some other time, in what terms to do it and in reproving

79

Show no Sign of Cholar but do it with all Sweetness and Mildness."

Commentary: Whether one is advising another or reprehending them, timing, terrain (i.e. location), and tone are essential dimensions of what is truly civil and stands a chance of being most effective. Furthermore, in almost inverse proportion, a message that is one of admonishment or reproach will best be received if done without a tone of accusation, but rather peacefulness. The "sweetness and mildness" referred to here should not come across as an affectation – which would be more of a passive-aggressive message. Again, if one holds in mind the Buddhist notion of basic goodness as an essential component of our human nature, to respond in this way is less effortful and more genuine.

46. "Take all Admonitions thankfully in what Time or Place Soever given but afterwards not being culpable take a Time and Place convenient to let him know it that gave them."

Commentary: Rule 45 provides some guidance on how to most skillfully and with civility offer advice or admonition. This does not mean, however, that those who admonish you may have the same thoughtfulness or consideration. Thus you may be embarrassed in front of others, which can be hurtful, degrading, etc... However, you should understand that vehemently defending oneself or challenging he or she who admonished you in the same venue, though seeming justified, will not necessarily be looked upon with favor by anyone, even those who wish you to defend yourself. Thus it is with patience and concerted effort that if one needs to correct an accusation or judgment falsely made, you should apply the time, terrain, and tone recommendations of Rule 45. Doing so will put you in a greater light with your accuser who may, in fact, then go out of their way to make their misjudgment or mistake known to others. In the long run, your civil approach may be a far greater method in being exonerated than going on the defensive.

47. "Mock not nor Jest at any thing of Importance, break no Jest that are Sharp Biting, and if you Deliver any nothing witty and Pleasant abstain from Laughing thereat yourself."

Commentary: Whether the matter being attended to is of utmost or relative importance with the person or persons with whom you are engaged, you should be mindful not to trivialize or turn whatever it may be into some kind of joke. Of course, there may be a humorous or light side to what is being addressed, but this is holding the topic or issue as dear and finding something in it that may help ease tensions or even allow for more candid discussion to emerge. Then again, if in the mind of those others the matter is a "sacred cow," more than likely they will not be able to endure even a lighter side to the matter. With wit that is sharp tongued, the delivery of such is usually of a serious nature – possibly even an affront. Thus whether it is you who delivers it or it is offered by another, a mirthful or light jesting tone will actually seem more cruel and/or insensitive. And lastly, if it is you who are offering the jest or the mirth, to laugh at it yourself is to put your wit into the category of self-indulgent entertainment. It actually degrades the value of the jest or point being lightly made.

48. "Wherein you reprove Another be unblameable yourself; for example is more prevalent than Precepts."

Commentary: The modern saying in more colloquial terms is: "People in glass houses shouldn't throw stones."

However, if you can be blamed for the same as you are making accusations of, have you experienced and made a reformation of character? In such a case, you may be able to show more empathy for what the other is doing, but also be able to demonstrate that one can reform one's thoughts and actions, which in turn may actually be quite inspiring. This lesson is best demonstrated if one looks at parenting and/or mentoring as a maturing of our nature and character. However, it is obvious that if one has not reformed oneself and is still practicing the offending behavior, etc., then such hypocrisy will make the accusation fall on deaf ears and possibly be a cause supportive for future bad behavior. There is the story of a woman who brought her son to Gandhi and asked Gandhi-ji to tell her son to stop eating sugar. Gandhi said nothing to the son, but told her to bring her son back in a week. When she returned with her son, Gandhi looked at her son and said, "Stop eating sugar." She then enquired, "Why did you not say that last week?" He replied, "Because last week I was still eating sugar myself."

49. "Use no Reproachful Language against any one; neither Curse nor Revile."

    Commentary: There is a difference between using language that reproaches a person's actions versus base language that is directed at their personage.

50. "Be not hasty to believe flying Reports to the Disparagement of any."

    Commentary: A skilled mind that holds as true our basic goodness is less susceptible to any reactive commentary. In actual fact, it is sometimes hyperbolic compliments, which bypass our wariness, that create worse or more problematic results.

51. "Wear not your Cloths foul, ripped or dusty, but See

they be brushed once every day at least and take heed that you approach to any Uncleanliness."

Commentary: Dignity is demonstrated in the efforts to make one as presentable as is possible. To be in the company with others who hold to such is to elevate one's own sense of such. By the same token, if one has need or circumstance that places one in the company of those less fortunate and/or unclean, your example can be inspiring.

52. "In your Apparel, be Modest and endeavor to accommodate Nature, rather than to procure Admiration; Keep to the Fashion of your equals, such as are Civil and orderly with respect to Times and Places."

Commentary: Don't make a spectacle of yourself unless the circumstance is intended for all to do so, i.e. for a ball, party, etc... Otherwise, your vanity will prove a distraction to your character and intent. Furthermore, be aware of the circumstance, time, place, and convention when you consider what to wear.

53. "Run not in the Streets, neither go too slowly nor with Mouth open; Go not Shaking your Arms, kick not the earth with your feet, go not upon the Toes, nor in a Dancing fashion."

Commentary: Such a Rule emphasizes the breeding and station of those who certainly had the ability to be literate in the time in which these Rules were written. But, it is a general reminder to know your place and take in to consideration the perception of others who you hold in esteem, your equals, even those who you may consider socially lesser who look to you as an example.

54. "Play not the Peacock, looking every where about you, to See is you be well Decked, if your Shoes fit well, if your Stockings sit neatly, and Cloths handsomely."

Commentary: Vanity is an affect. To present oneself in an affective way demonstrates a shallowness of character.

55. "Eat not in the Streets, nor in the House, out of Season."
Commentary: In a time of intact families and the proper times and places to eat, such a Rule seems antiquated if not out of step with the hustle and mayhem of modern culture. Yet, regulation in the time and place of eating creates regularity both socially and biologically. Without such, the graze or snack mentality of eating, in the home, on the street, on the bus, etc. is a sign of a culture out of touch with biological needs and oblivious to or ignoring of the consequences that this creates on many levels of our psycho-socio-biological existence. Civility, propriety, and decorum are best served when we are in touch with what nurtures us on a day-to-day basis.

56. "Associate yourself with Men of good Quality if you Esteem your own Reputation; for it is better to be alone than in bad company."
Commentary: As Hawkins' book was written with young men in mind, such a recommendation, the emphasis of this Rule, is on mentorship and being among those who set the kind of example you want to live up to in the future. At the same time, once one has risen to that stature and become a man or person of good quality in the eyes of others, one then may indeed associate with those deemed lesser or in search of mentors, like the kind you may have, indeed, become.

57. "In walking up and down in a House only with One in Company, if he be Greater than yourself, at the first give him the Right hand, and Stop not till he does, and be not the first that turns, and when you do turn let it be with your face towards him, if he be a Man of Great Quality,

walk not with him Cheek by Jowl but Somewhat behind him; but yet in Such a Manner that he may easily Speak to you."

Commentary: Manners matter and, indeed, there are still teachers of such to this day. None of what is said is really antiquated, just so rarely observed. Other than showing respect for elders and those perceived as worthy of such, such actions provide the maximum opportunity to stay engaged in presence and conversation.

58. "Let your Conversation be without Malice or Envy, for 'tis a Sign of a Tractable and Commendable Nature: And in all Causes of Passion admit Reason to Govern."

Commentary: Conversation governed by baser emotions of ill intent rarely engenders trust or admiration. Conversely, even when engaging with others who display such or others contending with those heaping upon them malice or envy, to stay "above the fray," letting your reason govern the conversation and keeping your passions within due bounds engender trust and admiration.

59. "Never express anything unbecoming, nor Act against the Rules Moral before your inferiors."

Commentary: When someone holds you in deference, the weight of what you say has a stronger impact. Thus while amongst equals or those who you perceive of a more noble nature, you stand a better chance of being understood in a better context and if admonition for your words are warranted, then you should be willing to accept them as a lesson of right speech. Refer to the section on the Buddha's words on Proper Speech in Chapter Three.

60. "Be not immodest in urging your Friends to Discover a Secret."

Commentary: Being eager to discover what another

wishes concealed attracts suspicions of your motives. Furthermore, it is setting up others to do your "dirty work" and may even jeopardize their station and reputation.

61. "Utter not base and frivolous things amongst grave and Learned Men; nor very Difficult Questions or Subjects among the Ignorant, or things hard to be believed; Stuff not your Discourse with Sentences amongst your Betters or Equals."

Commentary: In the Lojong Slogans of Atisha cited in the preceding section, Slogan 37 is "Don't turn Gods into Demons." Regarding the first point in this Rule, don't degrade the conversation or your relationship with people of quality by wasting their time and energy on base or frivolous matters. Amongst those who have lesser capacity than you, don't burden or try to impress them with matters that will only confuse or lead to harm in some way. And lastly, avoid excess verbosity in conversing with your equals or those you deem with esteem.

62. "Speak not of doleful Things in a Time of Mirth or at the Table; Speak not of Melancholy Things as Death and Wounds, and if others Mention them Change if you can the Discourse; Tell not your Dreams, but to your intimate Friend."

Commentary: Know the context and pay attention to the mood of the conversation and setting, irrespective of topic. In particular, to bring up what most see as dire topics requires a time and timing and context where people can be prepared to receive such. With respect to dreams, as they are generally of a personal nature, unless you are in a circle friends to who this is of interest, to share such with a limited number of close friends is the best context for such to be revealed.

63. "A Man ought not to value himself of his achievements, or rare Qualities of wit, much less of his Riches, Virtue, or Kindred."

Commentary: Self-flattery or pride over one's own status, etc. is boorish.

64. "Break not a Jest where none take pleasure in mirth; Laugh not aloud, nor at all without Occasion; Deride no man's Misfortune, though there Seem to be Some cause."

Commentary: Again, pay attention. But, beyond just paying attention, become sensitive to the social environment of which you are a part. When it comes to others and their misfortunes, if we truly believe that everyone possesses a loving nature, to act in a manner that shows happiness for another's sorrows – even if you think they are warranted – reflects badly on your own character. Regarding the point on laughter, we are strangely in a digital age where people may be plugged into a conversation or event on their media of which we know nothing. Thus we watch angry outbursts, laughter, seemingly strange comments be uttered that we do not know the context of. How much does this make us "tune-out" their actions and voices? How much does it impact what we think about these people?

65. "Speak not injurious Words, neither in Jest nor Earnest Scoff none although they give Occasion."

Commentary: Just because someone sets himself or herself up for ridicule or derision, does not mean that one should take advantage of this situation. In fact, to do so will only make you smaller in the eyes of not only the person themselves, but others watching you do so.

66. "Be not forward but friendly and Courteous; the first to Salute, hear, and answer and be not Pensive when it's time to Converse."

Commentary: To be too eager or reserved or seemingly distant from being able to be engaged requires an attentive, peaceful mind ready to engage, or not. How present are you to those who are present to you?

67. "Detract not from others, neither be excessive in Commanding."

Commentary: How well do you stand out of the way to allow others to have their just due in company, etc.? Learn not to deflect one towards yourself, interrupt, or try to make yourself more than the other to whom the conversation is directed. Even if you need to be commanding in the circumstance, try not to let your action seem too forward or pushy as you may be met with more resistance or resentment than is necessary to get done what needs to be done.

68. "Go not thither, where you know not whether you Shall be Welcome or not. Give not Advice without being Asked, and when desired do it briefly."

Commentary: In a mass transit and personal transportation world, it is hard to conceive of a time when most people did not travel more than five miles from their own dwelling or town. Other than explorers, adventurers or other vagabonds, there was far less awareness and/or certainty of what one might find beyond the normal limits of the day. Now, we get in our cars or get on a bus and cruise or tour, window shop, etc... We may take for granted the safety of such and it is not to say that the world (that most of us live in) is a dangerous place. But, if we were more measured in our actions, travelled only when necessary rather than as part of our entertainment, how would this change our perception as to what is of necessity in travelling? How would this redefine our sense of home and place?

The second portion of this Rule could be looked at in the

context of going to a place where you are perhaps not known or welcome. In this light, it makes only sense not to come out too forward with what you think, but wait for the request of your words or advice to be asked for.

69. "If two contend together, take not the part of either unconstrained; and be not obstinate in your own Opinion, in Things indifferent be of the Major Side."

Commentary: If you are in a situation where two people are having a contentious interaction, if you feel the need to take sides, do so with caution and not to make your opinion stronger than the argument of the person you are siding with. And if there are more than two and the matter is trivial or it really doesn't matter as far as you are concerned, then just go with the majority as this will make the matter move along more smoothly.

70. "Reprehend not the imperfections of others for that belongs to Parents, masters, and Superior."

Commentary: When you know that someone has been raised or mentored in mannerisms and speech that are unskillful, it is far better to approach them with kindness and endeavor to bring about a reformation. As nature will always win out over nurturing, by appealing to their basic goodness rather than that in which they have been conditioned, one may see a change, which brings more light into their lives, hence affecting others as well. As this situation is more than not the case, it is a good general practice.

71. "Gaze not on the marks or blemishes of Others, and ask not how they came. What you may Speak in Secret to your Friend deliver not before others."

Commentary: These can be looked at together or separately. The first part of this Rule reminds one of the saying, "There but for the grace of God go I." As mentioned previously, within us, there are mirror neurons. They are situated behind our heart and communicate with our brain and more signals go from our hearts to our brains than vice versa. Thus, when we see the presence of suffering, whether it be an act or the appearance of such in the flesh, we do feel it, perhaps get even shocked by it. This may elicit various responses other than sympathy or empathy, mostly negative in nature and often driven by fear. Thus, other than the good manners to not comment on blemishes, etc., to deepen one's calm and clarity in order not to project shock, fear, or avoidance, examine within yourself how you are affected by it. In that way, your response becomes more natural.

Of course, you may comment to a friend in secret about this. But to then spread that "secret" about is to turn such into gossip – which one should examine oneself for doing.

72. "Speak not in an unknown Tongue in Company, but in your own Language, and that as those of Quality do and not as the vulgar; Sublime matters treat Seriously."
Commentary: To speak in a language that others do not understand can be taken in many ways, but usually does not reflect positively on the one doing such. A display of superiority, an attempt to overtly exclude some…? Thus, speak the language that is common to you and your company, and do so in a way that demonstrates a respect for the communication in which you are engaged. Furthermore, when it comes to more religious, philosophical, or spiritual matters, to belittle, mock, mention them casually or make them somehow ordinary often is seen less as clever, but rather offensive to greater or lesser degree.

73. "Think before you Speak; pronounce not imperfectly nor bring your Words too hastily, but orderly and

distinctly."

Commentary: All good advice to demonstrate that whatever you are saying comes from a degree of consideration. That it is not forced also provides whomever you are conversing with the opportunity to respond in a like (considered) manner.

74. "When Another Speaks, be attentive your Self and disturb not the Audience. If any hesitate in his Words, help him nor Prompt him without desired; Interrupt him not, nor Answer him till his Speech be ended."

Commentary: A Rule of respect. Also, when a person forgets a word or pauses to clarify or add to what they have said, rarely do they want unsolicited help. Furthermore, though it may be tempting to answer or comment when you think you know what they mean or what they are asking, again, like in Rule 73, to not be hasty allows for the conversation to flow more comfortably without undue urgency.

75. "In the midst of Discourse, ask not of what one treateth; but if you Perceive any Stop because of your coming you may well in treat him gently to Proceed; If a Person of Quality comes in while you're Conversing, it's handsome to Repeat what was said before."

Commentary: If someone is speaking and you happen to come into the room or join them in a conversation they are having with another, do not ask them to repeat what they have said. But, if there is a natural pause when you arrive, you may ask them to continue, which they may want to or not, but is completely up to them. By the same token, if a person of note comes up to you and those you are conversing with, it is respectful to repeat what has been said as a recap if you think the situation warrants it and/or will make them feel more comfortable and in the flow of the conversing.

76. "While you are talking, Point not with your Finger at him of Whom you Discourse nor Approach too near him to whom you talk, especially to his face."

    Commentary: Such actions or gestures are often felt as threatening, either overtly or covertly. In civil discourse, you should take note of this.

77. "Treat with men at fit Times about Business and Whisper not in the Company of Others."

    Commentary: Timing does matter. Whatever the nature of the business, choose to converse or engage in it when the time to do so seems appropriate. It is a good practice to be aware that each of us needs times of silence and reflection, times to work, times for service to others who may need our assistance, and times for refreshment and repose. To keep such times clearly delineated makes for a more harmonious life. And with respect to whispering, to do so in public makes others feel excluded and may even incur suspicion – even if it is not warranted.

78. "Make no Comparison, and if any of the Company be Commended for any brave act of Virtue, commend not another for the Same."

    Commentary: If someone is being praised or commended, to decide to mention another will naturally make people draw a comparison, in which case, the credit to both may be lost. The phrase, not "to rain on someone's parade..." seems apt.

79. "Be not apt to relate News if you know not the truth thereof. In Discoursing of things you Have heard, Name not your Author always. A Secret Discover not."

    Commentary: Passing on what you are unsure of can generate gossip and jeopardizes your credibility. Furthermore, if you do know something that is verifiable but comes from another, be discreet. Do they want to be known or would they prefer for them being the source to remain secret?

80. "Be not Tedious in Discourse or in reading unless you find the Company pleased therewith."

Commentary: Pay attention to how people are receiving what you are saying. It may even be that what you are saying is of lesser consequence to your audience than the fact that you are saying it!

81. "Be not Curious to Know the Affairs of Others neither approach those that Speak in Private."

Commentary: As curiosity arises emotionally, it is difficult for it not to be there when it is. However, it then becomes a practice not to indulge in it when it comes to the private lives of others. By the same token, while the Rules speak to you, yourself, not speaking privately or in a secretive way when in the view or company of others, one cannot insist that others follow the same level of civility to not do it themselves. In such a situation, it is better to step back from it and let whatever is transpiring to transpire, knowing that if those doing so want you to be in the know, you will learn of it soon enough.

82. "Undertake not what you cannot Perform, but be Careful to keep your Promise."

Commentary: A paradoxical combination. It is a good practice to know yourself well enough to know, understand, and not exceed your own capabilities. This is in the normal course of things. To practice stretching oneself to grow as such is not discouraged, but especially in situations where a result is expected or the stakes are high, better to decline or defer to another. However, once you have promised to do something, then you place yourself in a situation where, in fact, stretching yourself is what you are expected to do. Even if you fail, in the face of a promise, it is better to be seen in the effort of trying than in cowering or avoiding altogether. In a sense, embarrassment is far better than being seen as untrustworthy or not of your word.

83. "When you deliver a matter, do it without Passion and with Discretion, however mean the Person be you do it to."

Commentary: By "matter," it would appear that Hawkins is speaking of an issue that you need to bring before another. The recommendation is to be factual and respectful, providing what needs to be known without adding to it your own emotionality. Then, even if the situation is unpleasant, the facts, rather than your emotionality, are what the other will be led to focus on without deflection.

84. "When your Superiors talk to any Body, hearken not neither Speak nor Laugh."

Commentary: It is clear in this Rule that Hawkins is addressing young men who need to develop a proper relationship to their "superiors." However, even in the course of one person addressing another specifically, it is better not to make yourself part of what needs to be considered. Even if this is in a group setting, there will be dyadic conversing where the commentary of others is unwarranted, unwelcome, or simply superfluous to the transaction.

85. "In Company of these of Higher Quality than yourself, Speak not 'til you are asked a Question; then Stand upright, put off your Hat and Answer in few words."

Commentary: In a world and time of aristocracy and those of a younger age learning to find their place, these comments are direct and obvious. But, in everyday life, where there are people of note and those whom we venerate for whatever reason, these comments create a civil and orderly process in the flow of communication.

In a world lapsing into a perpetual casual culture, such an approach may seem stiff and stultifying. But, it is amazing to see how easily the flow of ideas and actions go when such Rules are given heed.

86. "In Disputes, be not So Desirous to Overcome as not to give Liberty to each other to deliver his Opinion; and Submit to the Judgment of the Major Part, especially if they are Judges of the Dispute."

Commentary: Do not be overbearing in expressing your opinion and give each person their due. Here, Hawkins, in speaking to young men, encourages them to bend to the majority or the judges of disputed issues. Thus, there is little said to train one to be young, civil, and yet rebellious. Using some of the wisdom of the Buddha to assist in such matters is warranted per the descriptions of speech and harmonious societies written of in the earlier section of this book.

87. "Let they carriage be such as becomes a Man: Grave, Settled, and Attentive to that which is spoken. Contradict not at every turn what others Say."

Commentary: As if knowing that some of a younger age may take exception to following Rule 86 to the letter, in the latter half of this Rule, he explains that if you are going to be contrary, don't make it a style just for the sake of it. If you are grave, settled, and attentive, then if you do have to contradict, it will be well measured and, more than likely, appropriately delivered.

88. "Be not tedious in Discourse, make not many Digressions, nor repeat often the same manner of Discourse."

Commentary: Don't be redundant, nor take people down various side issues that may have little relevance to what you are trying to put across. And if the same issues or points need to be made, be measured how and when a repeat of such is delivered, lest your repetitions themselves become regarded as tedious and bothersome.

89. "Speak not Evil of the absent, for it is unjust."

Commentary: In the Buddhist understanding of the world, there is nothing that is purely evil. There are just gradations of confusion that lead to unskillful words and actions. Thus to speak evil of another is basically uncalled for, although commentary on actions, words, and behavior seen as suspect, dangerous, etc. may well be warranted. Sometimes these things need to be discussed. But, when it comes to admonishing another and desiring a reformation of their character or person, it is far better that they are present, in the final analysis and when the time is deemed appropriate. Otherwise, the conversation about them will sour into gossip of the most upsetting and poisonous sort.

In general, Rules 90 through 107 are about propriety in eating and dining etiquette. In times when the day began at sunrise and ended at nightfall, dining together was a central feature of instilling harmony in the family and meeting of others outside the functions of work or religious activity. It was clearly understood that the raising and harvesting of one's food was a core feature of a civilized community. Understanding this very basic fact of life and appreciating it for the nurturing it offers on many levels was more commonplace than it is today.

With respect to etiquette in particular, one could see the upbringing, demeanor, and civil disposition in how one approached food and showed consideration for those around the dining table. If meal times and getting together to eat as families became commonplace, again, how would that effect family life and relations – especially if no one could bring their cell phone or other personal device to the table?!

90. "Set at meat, Scratch not, neither Spit, Cough, or blow

your Nose, except there's a Necessity for it."

Commentary: Common decency when dining with others.

91. "Make no Show of taking great Delight in your Victuals, Feed not with Greediness; cut your Bread with a Knife, lean not on then Table, neither find fault with what you Eat."

Commentary: In these modern times when many people eat out, snack, or graze more frequently than actually sit down with others to "break bread" in any formal or familial way, the social graces of healthy, respectable, and gracious dining are all but lost. And yet, business luncheons and lunches are not infrequent as a part of commerce, conversing over deals, etc... Thus the manners and mindfulness of eating bear paying attention to as one more avenue in which one demonstrates a civil approach to an important human function and venue of social discourse.

92. "Take no Salt or cut Bread with your Knife Greasy."

Commentary: More than likely this Rule has less to do with hygiene than it does about using implements that are definitely yours by their use and applying them to what is commonly shared. It may be considered not unlike an animal "tagging" something for themselves.

93. "Entertaining any one at the Table, it is decent to present them with meat; undertake not to help others undesired by the Master."

Commentary: In this case the "Master" may be a father or whoever is deemed head of the table. In the perspective of such a hierarchy, Hawkins advises one not to invite someone to the table if you know that he or she are not acceptable to the head of the table. And, if they are, be sure that they are served like anyone and everyone else who is at the table.

94. "If you Soak bread in the Sauce, let it be no more than what you put in your Mouth at a time; and blow not your broth at Table but Stay till (it) Cools of itself."

Commentary: If you soak more than one mouthful, you will be holding a drippy piece of bread. Regarding hot soup or broths, those of manners learn that if you scoop along the edge where the liquid meets the bowl on the surface, you will find the mouthful cooled down enough.

95. "Put not your meat to your Mouth with your Knife in your hand, neither Spit forth the stones of any fruit Pie upon a Dish, nor Cast anything under the table."

Commentary: It would be interesting to learn when the idea of cutting one's meat or other food, putting down the knife, then using the fork to eat the portion began. It is now a more common American cutlery habit compared to the European style where both fork and knife are employed. And, if stones from a pie with stoned fruit cannot be put on a plate and you can't toss it under the table, is it to be placed in a napkin?

96. "It's unbecoming to Stoop much to one's Meat. Keep your Fingers clean and when foul wipe them on a Corner of your Table Napkin."

Commentary: A healthy, upright posture shows breeding, improves digestion, and reduces the likelihood of mess or spills.

97. "Put not another bit into your mouth 'till the former be swallowed. Let not your morsels be too big for the jowls."

Commentary: The art of proper chewing, both in size and number of chews per bite, is not only good etiquette, but makes digestive sense from the standpoint of ensuring that food swallowed does not lead to hiccups, unnecessary belching, flatulence and other manifestations of digestive distress.

98. "Drink not nor talk with your mouth full; neither gaze about you while you are drinking."

    Commentary: Presumably, both aspects of this rule are to ensure that you look composed while eating, but also do not inadvertently spray or spill on others.

99. "Drink not too leisurely nor yet too hastily. Before and after drinking, wipe your lips; breath not then or ever with too great a noise, for its uncivil."

    Commentary: Composure creates a context in which others are engaged in a state of greater ease and receptivity for civil discourse.

100. "Cleanse not your teeth with the table cloth napkin, fork, or knife; but if others do it, let it be done without a peep to them."

    Commentary: Mind your own manners as such and make no comment to others, lest to make a spectacle of their improprieties, which will cause embarrassment and/or annoyance.

101. "Rinse not your mouth in the presence of others."
    Commentary: Such a behavior is best done in private or in a bathroom.

102. "It is out of use to call upon the company often to eat; nor need you drink to others every time you drink."

    Commentary: Although to do these acts is a custom of courtesy, know your situation, the time, and the timing. To act reflexively or habitually in such matters will usually create awkward moments, which may be perceived as token or insincere.

103. "In the company of your betters, be not longer in eating than they are; lay not your arm but only your hand upon the table."

    Commentary: To linger longer when eating puts you in the situation of setting the timing and pace of the dining situation, which could be considered lazy or disrespectful to those who one should defer to. Also, to place one's arm on the table may be seen as a sign of laziness, a casual attitude, or impropriety.

104. "It belongs to the chiefest in company to unfold his napkin and fall to meat first, but he ought then to begin in time and to dispatch with dexterity that the slowest may have time allowed him."

Commentary: A sign of a truly quality leader, patron, or "chiefest" person is that they have a natural and/or due consideration for everyone at the table so that no person feels lesser or embarrassed unduly, regardless of their standing.

105. "Be not angry at the table, whatever happens; and if you have reason to be so, show it not; put on a cheerful countenance especially if there be strangers, for good humor makes one dish of meat a feast."

Commentary: Nothing ruins a meal faster than anger and other negative emotions people are feeling and/or displaying while trying to eat. Try to clear the air, let it go. Breathing deeply and calmly, like in meditation. And if you cannot contain yourself, it is better to excuse yourself than to infect the dining experience of others.

106. "Set not yourself at the upper of the table; but if it be your due or that the master of the house will have it so, contend not, least you should trouble the company."

Commentary: It is not your place to choose the head of the table as yours unless it is so. However, when the master or company offer you that spot, you should accept their generosity. In Buddhist thinking, it is always beneficial to the one offering generosity for one to accept it from them.

107. "If others talk at the table, be attentive but talk not with meat in your mouth."

Commentary: Do not let your haste to respond make a display of the content of your mouth. By allowing chewing to set the pace, your words will be far better considered, presented, and more than likely received.

The final three Rules are general recommendations covering the more basic and spiritual dimensions of our lives and are the prerequisites for being able to enact a life of civility for the betterment and benefit of all.

108. "When you speak of God or his attributes, let it be seriously and with reverence. Honor and obey your natural parents although they be poor."

Commentary: When it comes to the spiritual dimension of our nature and our attitude towards the transcendent, we should treat such matters with reverence. Like the Slogan of Atisha, which mentions not bringing "gods down to demons," an attitude arising from an appreciation and reverence of such brings out our best, even if our best is not even what we have in mind for ourselves. The last point, about our birth parents, is reiterated in Buddhism, which speaks of the unconditional love parents, especially mothers, have for their offspring. Even if they are not wealthy or educated, and even if they were cruel or unskillful in other ways, consider that without their care day to day in keeping one fed, protected from the environment and dangerous influences, we would not have the life and opportunity we have here and now. (Of note: the number 108 is significant in terms of the rosary, the prayer beads of Buddhists, and even is representative of other transcendent realities. That Hawkins, therefore, makes these points in Rule 108 should not be viewed as mere happenstance.)

109. "Let your recreations be manful, not sinful."

Commentary: Although this comment is made with

respect to gender, the basic point is to participate and enjoy recreation that is energizing and rewarding, be it more athletic or sedentary in nature. "Sinful" recreation has more to do with what is base and somehow destructive personally, collectively, morally.

110. "Labor to keep alive in your breast that little spark of celestial fire called conscience."

Commentary: This is in alignment with the Buddhist notion of basic goodness. Hawkins sees the celestial fire as a part of our very nature. But like basic goodness, without training, discipline, and mindfulness it is easy to lapse into habitual behaviors that serve neither us nor the world in which we live.

This final Rule is a fitting end to the Rules and to this book. May it support and uplift all beings to live more civil lives in harmony with others near and far.

Appendix: Mind Training Slogans

(From: Wikipedia)

The original Lojong practice consists of 59 slogans, or aphorisms. These slogans are further organized into seven groupings, called the "7 Points of Lojong". The categorized slogans are listed below, translated by the Nalanda Translation Committee under the direction of Chögyam Trungpa.[8] The following is translated from ancient Sanskrit and Tibetan texts and may vary slightly from other translations. Many contemporary gurus and experts have written extensive commentaries elucidating the Lojong text and slogans.

Point One: The preliminaries, which are the basis for dharma practice

Slogan 1. First, train in the preliminaries; The four reminders,[9] or alternatively called the Four Thoughts.[10]

1. Maintain an awareness of the preciousness of human life.
2. Be aware of the reality that life ends; death comes for everyone; Impermanence.
3. Recall that whatever you do, whether virtuous or not, has a result; Karma.
4. Contemplate that as long as you are too focused on self-importance and too caught up in thinking about how you are good or bad, you will experience suffering. Obsessing about getting what you want and avoiding what you don't want does not result in happiness; Ego.

Point Two: The main practice, which is training in bodhicitta

Absolute Bodhicitta

Slogan 2. Regard all dharmas as dreams; although experiences may seem solid, they are passing memories.

Slogan 3. Examine the nature of unborn awareness.

Slogan 4. Self-liberate even the antidote.

Slogan 5. Rest in the nature of alaya, the essence, the present moment.

Slogan 6. In postmeditation, be a child of illusion.

Relative Bodhicitta

Slogan 7. Sending and taking should be practiced alternately. These two should ride the breath (aka practice Tonglen).

Slogan 8. Three objects, three poisons, three roots of virtue – The 3 objects are friends, enemies and neutrals. The 3 poisons are craving, aversion and indifference. The 3 roots of virtue are the remedies.

Slogan 9. In all activities, train with slogans.

Slogan 10. Begin the sequence of sending and taking with yourself.

Point Three: Transformation of Bad Circumstances into the Way of Enlightenment

Slogan 11. When the world is filled with evil, transform all mishaps into the path of bodhi.

Slogan 12. Drive all blames into one.

Slogan 13. Be grateful to everyone.

Slogan 14. Seeing confusion as the four kayas is unsurpassable shunyata protection.

The kayas are Dharmakaya, sambhogakaya, nirmanakaya, svabhavikakaya. Thoughts have no birthplace, thoughts are unceasing, thoughts are not solid, and these three characteristics are interconnected. Shunyata can be described as "complete openness."

Slogan 15. Four practices are the best of methods.

The four practices are: accumulating merit, laying down evil deeds, offering to the dons, and offering to the dharmapalas.

Slogan 16. Whatever you meet unexpectedly, join with meditation.

Point Four: Showing the Utilization of Practice in One's Whole Life

Slogan 17. Practice the five strengths, the condensed heart instructions.

The 5 strengths are: strong determination, familiarization, the positive seed, reproach, and aspiration.

Slogan 18. The mahayana instruction for ejection of consciousness at death is the five strengths: how you conduct yourself is important.

When you are dying practice the 5 strengths.

Point Five: Evaluation of Mind Training

Slogan 19. All dharma agrees at one point – All Buddhist teachings are about lessening the ego, lessening one's self-absorption.

Slogan 20. Of the two witnesses, hold the principal one – You know yourself better than anyone else knows you.

Slogan 21. Always maintain only a joyful mind.

Slogan 22. If you can practice even when distracted, you are well trained.

Point Six: Disciplines of Mind Training

Slogan 23. Always abide by the three basic principles – Dedication to your practice, refraining from outrageous conduct, developing patience.

Slogan 24. Change your attitude, but remain natural. Reduce ego clinging, but be yourself.

Slogan 25. Don't talk about injured limbs – Don't take pleasure contemplating others' defects.

Slogan 26. Don't ponder others – Don't take pleasure contemplating others' weaknesses.

Slogan 27. Work with the greatest defilements first – Work with your greatest obstacles first.

Slogan 28. Abandon any hope of fruition – Don't get caught up in how you will be in the future, stay in the present moment.

Slogan 29. Abandon poisonous food.

Slogan 30. Don't be so predictable – Don't hold grudges.

Slogan 31. Don't malign others.

Slogan 32. Don't wait in ambush – Don't wait for others' weaknesses to show to attack them.

Slogan 33. Don't bring things to a painful point – Don't humiliate others.

Slogan 34. Don't transfer the ox's load to the cow – Take responsibility for yourself.

Slogan 35. Don't try to be the fastest – Don't compete with others.

Slogan 36. Don't act with a twist – Do good deeds without scheming about benefiting yourself.

Slogan 37. Don't turn gods into demons – Don't use these slogans or your spirituality to increase your self-absorption.

Slogan 38. Don't seek others' pain as the limbs of your own happiness.

Slogan 39. All activities should be done with one intention.

Slogan 40. Correct all wrongs with one intention.

Slogan 41. Two activities: one at the beginning, one at the end.

Slogan 42. Whichever of the two occurs, be patient.

Slogan 43. Observe these two, even at the risk of your life.

Slogan 44. Train in the three difficulties.

Slogan 45. Take on the three principal causes: the teacher, the dharma, the sangha.

Slogan 46. Pay heed that the three never wane: gratitude

towards one's teacher, appreciation of the dharma (teachings) and correct conduct.

Slogan 47. Keep the three inseparable: body, speech, and mind.

Slogan 48. Train without bias in all areas. It is crucial always to do this pervasively and wholeheartedly.

Slogan 49. Always meditate on whatever provokes resentment.

Slogan 50. Don't be swayed by external circumstances.

Slogan 51. This time, practice the main points: others before self, dharma, and awakening compassion.

Slogan 52. Don't misinterpret.

The six things that may be misinterpreted are patience, yearning, excitement, compassion, priorities and joy. You're patient when you're getting your way, but not when it's difficult. You yearn for worldly things, instead of an open heart and mind. You get excited about wealth and entertainment, instead of your potential for enlightenment. You have compassion for those you like, but none for those you don't. Worldly gain is your priority rather than cultivating loving-kindness and compassion. You feel joy when your enemies suffer, and do not rejoice in others' good fortune.[1]

Slogan 53. Don't vacillate (in your practice of LoJong).

Slogan 54. Train wholeheartedly.

Slogan 55. Liberate yourself by examining and analyzing: Know your own mind with honesty and fearlessness.

Slogan 56. Don't wallow in self-pity.

Slogan 57. Don't be jealous.

Slogan 58. Don't be frivolous.

Slogan 59. Don't expect applause.

Endnotes

Introduction

1. David McCullough, *1776*, p. 42

Chapter Two

2. Robert Sachs, *The Wisdom of the Buddhist Masters: Common and Uncommon Sense*. Watkins, 2008

Chapter Three

3. Bhikkhu Bodhi, *The Buddha's Teachings on Social and Communal Harmony*, p. 77, AN 3:67
4. Bhikkhu Bodhi, *The Buddha's Teachings on Social and Communal Harmony*, p. 79
5. Majjhima Nikaya 139, found in *The Buddha's Teachings...*, Bodhi, p. 81
6. Anguttara Nikaya 5:167, *The Buddha's Teachings...*, Bodhi, p. 82

Selected Bibliography

Anderson-Smith and Various. *The Power of Civility*. San Francisco, CA: Thrive Publishing, 2011.

Bodhi, Bhikkhu. *The Buddha's Teachings on Social and Communal Harmony: An Anthology of Discourses from the Pali Canon.* Somerville, MA: Wisdom Publications, 2016.

Dunning, CR. *Contemplative Masonry*. Plano, Texas: Stone Guild Publishing, 2016.

McCullough, David. *1776*. New York: Simon and Schuster, 2005.

Sachs, Robert. *The Wisdom of the Buddhist Masters: Common and Uncommon Sense*. London: Watkins Publishing, 2008.

Sachs, Robert. *Becoming Buddha: Awakening the Wisdom and Compassion to Change Your World*. London: Watkins Publishing, 2010.

Sachs, Robert. *The Ecology of Oneness: Awakening in a Free World*. Bloomington, Indiana: iUniverse, 2016.

Shamar Rinpoche. *The Path to Awakening*. Delhi, India: Motilal Banarsidass, 2009.

Tabbert, Mark A. *George Washington's Rules for Freemasons in Life and Lodge*. Richmond, VA: Macoy Publishing and Masonic Supply Co., 2016.

Washington, George. *George Washington's Rules of Civility* (from Hawkins, Francis. *Youth's Behaviour, Or, Decencie in Conversation Amongst Men*, 1661). Alexandria, VA: The George Washington Masonic National Memorial Association.

Wikipedia Entry: on "Lojong."

About the author

Robert Sachs is a Licensed Clinical Social Worker, a licensed massage therapist, yoga instructor, and author. He has been a student of Indian and Tibetan spiritual and healing traditions since the early seventies. A Past Master of King David's Masonic Lodge #209 in San Luis Obispo, CA, he is also a 32nd degree Scottish Rite Mason and a trained mediator.

With his wife, Melanie, Robert co-owns and teaches for Diamond Way Ayurveda, the foremost promoters of Ayurveda in the spa and beauty industries. Along with their release, *Ayurvedic Spa*, Robert is the author of

Nine Star Ki: Feng Shui Astrology for Deepening Self-Knowledge and Enhancing Relationships, Health, and Prosperity
Tibetan Ayurveda: Health Secrets From The Roof of The World
Perfect Endings: A Conscious Approach to Dying and Death
The Passionate Buddha: Wisdom on Intimacy and Enduring Love
Becoming Buddha: Awakening the Wisdom and Compassion to Change Your World
The Wisdom of the Buddhist Masters: Common and Uncommon Sense
Rebirth Into Pure Land: A True Story of Birth, Death, and Transformation & How We Can Prepare for The Most Amazing Journey of Our Lives
The Ecology of Oneness: Awakening in a Free World
Start Your Day with a Good Night's Sleep
Psychic Whackos Save America

Robert lives with Melanie in Oceano, CA.

BOOKS

SPIRITUALITY

O is a symbol of the world, of oneness and unity; this eye represents knowledge and insight. We publish titles on general spirituality and living a spiritual life. We aim to inform and help you on your own journey in this life.
If you have enjoyed this book, why not tell other readers by posting a review on your preferred book site?
Recent bestsellers from O-Books are:

Heart of Tantric Sex

Diana Richardson

Revealing Eastern secrets of deep love and intimacy to Western couples.

Paperback: 978-1-90381-637-0 ebook: 978-1-84694-637-0

Crystal Prescriptions

The A-Z guide to over 1,200 symptoms and their healing crystals

Judy Hall

The first in the popular series of eight books, this handy little guide is packed as tight as a pill-bottle with crystal remedies for ailments.

Paperback: 978-1-90504-740-6 ebook: 978-1-84694-629-5

Take Me To Truth
Undoing the Ego
Nouk Sanchez, Tomas Vieira
The best-selling step-by-step book on shedding the Ego, using the teachings of *A Course In Miracles*.
Paperback: 978-1-84694-050-7 ebook: 978-1-84694-654-7

The 7 Myths about Love...Actually!
The Journey from your HEAD to the HEART of your SOUL
Mike George
Smashes all the myths about LOVE.
Paperback: 978-1-84694-288-4 ebook: 978-1-84694-682-0

The Holy Spirit's Interpretation of the New Testament
A Course in Understanding and Acceptance
Regina Dawn Akers
Following on from the strength of *A Course In Miracles*, NTI teaches us how to experience the love and oneness of God.
Paperback: 978-1-84694-085-9 ebook: 978-1-78099-083-5

The Message of A Course In Miracles
A translation of the Text in plain language
Elizabeth A. Cronkhite
A translation of *A Course in Miracles* into plain, everyday language for anyone seeking inner peace. The companion volume, *Practicing A Course In Miracles*, offers practical lessons and mentoring.
Paperback: 978-1-84694-319-5 ebook: 978-1-84694-642-4

Your Simple Path
Find Happiness in every step
Ian Tucker
A guide to helping us reconnect with what is really important in our lives.
Paperback: 978-1-78279-349-6 ebook: 978-1-78279-348-9

365 Days of Wisdom
Daily Messages To Inspire You Through The Year
Dadi Janki
Daily messages which cool the mind, warm the heart and guide you along your journey.
Paperback: 978-1-84694-863-3 ebook: 978-1-84694-864-0

Body of Wisdom
Women's Spiritual Power and How it Serves
Hilary Hart
Bringing together the dreams and experiences of women across the world with today's most visionary spiritual teachers.
Paperback: 978-1-78099-696-7 ebook: 978-1-78099-695-0

Dying to Be Free
From Enforced Secrecy to Near Death to True Transformation
Hannah Robinson
After an unexpected accident and near-death experience, Hannah Robinson found herself radically transforming her life, while a remarkable new insight altered her relationship with her father, a practising Catholic priest.
Paperback: 978-1-78535-254-6 ebook: 978-1-78535-255-3

The Ecology of the Soul
A Manual of Peace, Power and Personal Growth for Real People
in the Real World
Aidan Walker
Balance your own inner Ecology of the Soul to regain your
natural state of peace, power and wellbeing.
Paperback: 978-1-78279-850-7 ebook: 978-1-78279-849-1

Not I, Not other than I
The Life and Teachings of Russel Williams
Steve Taylor, Russel Williams
The miraculous life and inspiring teachings of one of the World's
greatest living Sages.
Paperback: 978-1-78279-729-6 ebook: 978-1-78279-728-9

On the Other Side of Love
A woman's unconventional journey towards wisdom
Muriel Maufroy
When life has lost all meaning, what do you do?
Paperback: 978-1-78535-281-2 ebook: 978-1-78535-282-9

Practicing A Course In Miracles
A translation of the Workbook in plain language, with mentor's
notes
Elizabeth A. Cronkhite
The practical second and third volumes of The Plain-Language
A Course In Miracles.
Paperback: 978-1-84694-403-1 ebook: 978-1-78099-072-9

Quantum Bliss

The Quantum Mechanics of Happiness, Abundance, and Health
George S. Mentz
Quantum Bliss is the breakthrough summary of success and
spirituality secrets that customers have been waiting for.
Paperback: 978-1-78535-203-4 ebook: 978-1-78535-204-1

The Upside Down Mountain

Mags MacKean
A must-read for anyone weary of chasing success and happiness
– one woman's inspirational journey swapping the uphill slog for
the downhill slope.
Paperback: 978-1-78535-171-6 ebook: 978-1-78535-172-3

Your Personal Tuning Fork

The Endocrine System
Deborah Bates
Discover your body's health secret, the endocrine system, and
'twang' your way to sustainable health!
Paperback: 978-1-84694-503-8 ebook: 978-1-78099-697-4

Readers of ebooks can buy or view any of these bestsellers by
clicking on the live link in the title. Most titles are published
in paperback and as an ebook. Paperbacks are available in
traditional bookshops. Both print and ebook formats are
available online.

Find more titles and sign up to our readers' newsletter at
http://www.johnhuntpublishing.com/mind-body-spirit

Follow us on Facebook at https://www.facebook.com/OBooks/
and Twitter at https://twitter.com/obooks